Kiddiwalks

IN
SURREY

David Weller

COUNTRYSIDE BOOKS
NEWBURY BERKSHIRE

COUNTRYSIDE BOOKS
3 Catherine Road
Newbury, Berkshire

To view our complete range of books,
please visit us at
www.countrysidebooks.co.uk

ISBN 1 85306 951 5
EAN 978185306 951 2

Designed by Peter Davies, Nautilus Design
Maps and photographs by the author
Cover picture supplied by Faith Tillotson

Produced through MRM Associates Ltd., Reading
Typeset by Mac Style, Nafferton, E. Yorkshire
Printed by Borcombe Printers plc, Romsey

Contents

Contents

PUBLISHER'S NOTE

We hope that you obtain considerable enjoyment from this book; great care has been taken in its preparation. Although at the time of publication all routes followed public rights of way or permitted paths, diversion orders can be made and permissions withdrawn.

We cannot, of course, be held responsible for such diversion orders and any inaccuracies in the text which result from these or any other changes to the routes nor any damage which might result from walkers trespassing on private property. We are anxious though that all details covering the walks are kept up to date and would therefore welcome information from readers which would be relevant to future editions.

The simple sketch maps that accompany the walks in this book are based on notes made by the author whilst checking out the routes on the ground. However, for the benefit of a proper map, we do recommend that you purchase the relevant Ordnance Survey sheet covering your walk. The Ordnance Survey maps are widely available, especially through booksellers and local newsagents.

AREA MAP SHOWING THE LOCATIONS OF THE WALKS

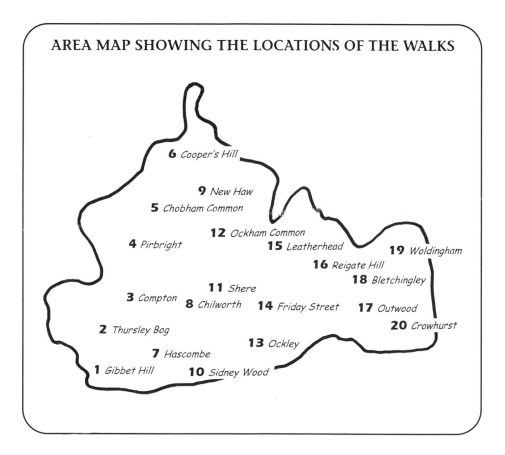

6 Cooper's Hill

9 New Haw
5 Chobham Common

12 Ockham Common
4 Pirbright **15** Leatherhead **19** Woldingham
16 Reigate Hill
18 Bletchingley
11 Shere
3 Compton **8** Chilworth **14** Friday Street **17** Outwood
2 Thursley Bog **20** Crowhurst
13 Ockley
7 Hascombe
1 Gibbet Hill **10** Sidney Wood

Introduction

Having had the good fortune to be brought up in a semi-rural part of Surrey more years ago than I wish to mention, and being able to wander through woods and fields without a care in the world, I realise now, on looking back, what an influence Surrey's wildlife and beautiful countryside have had on me.

The world has changed though and today's children are now necessarily kept under close parental supervision and can no longer roam at will. In these circuits, I have tried to inject some of the things I enjoyed doing as a child in the countryside, and each route has a unique feature for children, whether it is paddling in the clear waters of a stream, playing I-spy, spotting wildlife, identifying different species of tree or wildflower along the way or even creating a sculpture or Christmas decoration from leaves and fir cones found along the route.

I have rated each circuit for easiness and in a couple of instances I have made mention as to the suitability of the circuit for the passage of pushchairs. The sketch maps, with numbers that correspond to the numbered walk instructions, will guide you around the route but I do recommend that you also carry the relevant OS map, details of which are also given. These maps are particularly useful for identifying the main features of views. At the beginning of each circuit I have also recommended a local eatery that is reasonable and child friendly.

The circuits are generally well away from roads so children can run around to their hearts content and expel all their boundless energy, although caution should be taken, of course, on those routes that feature water. I would recommend that children wear long trousers to guard against the odd nettle sting and, of course, sensible shoes. I hope the whole family, especially the younger ones, will enjoy this collection of circular routes.

Now, gather up your children, make-up a mouth-watering picnic and go out there and enjoy our beautiful county and the adventures it contains.

David Weller

1

Gibbet Hill

The tale of the wicked sailors

The panoramic view from Gibbet Hill

This lovely walk starts on the rim of the Devil's Punchbowl and soon descends into Highcombe Bottom, a magical place at the foot of the escarpment and full of wildlife. After crossing a woodland brook, the way begins a steady climb out of the valley to reach the far side of the punchbowl where the route follows the old Portsmouth road. A very easy climb here brings you to the open hillside that was once known as Butterwedge Hill but now, since the infamous murder of a sailor in the 18th century, is called Gibbet Hill. Putting macabre thoughts to the back of your mind, enjoy the magnificent views the hill offers – some of the best in the south-east and a great picnic spot. Rejoining the old way, the circuit passes a memorial stone among the trees that marks the site of the crime and all too soon this great walk ends back at the café and car park.

Kiddiwalks in Surrey

1

Getting there *Take the A3 to Hindhead where just $^1/_4$ mile north of the traffic lights you will find the Devil's Punchbowl café and National Trust car park.*

Length of walk 2$^1/_2$ miles
Time Allow 1$^3/_4$ hours, more if picnicking.
Terrain Hilly but not too challenging for older children.
Start/Parking National Trust pay and display car park at the Devil's Punchbowl café (open 9 am to 9 pm) (GR 891358).

Map OS Landranger 186 Aldershot & Guildford, Camberley & Haslemere.
Refreshments The Devil's Punchbowl café makes a nice place to enjoy a cup of tea and a cake while the children enjoy their fizzy drinks and ice-creams.

❶ Leave the car park by crossing a picnic area to the right of the café and go down steps to meet a T-junction with a path on the rim of the Devil's Punchbowl. Turn left along a broad path that runs along the top of the rim and

◆ Fun Things to See and Do ◆

The walk is through woodland where there are many things to identify: birds, butterflies, ferns and wildflowers. See if you can also spot the strange things called oak apples that grow on the oak trees here. They are caused by gall wasps that lay their eggs on the trees; the tree then forms a growth around the larvae, unwittingly protecting it from predators. When developed the gall wasps, also known as gallflies, bore their way to the outside world and freedom.

Oak apples

The Walk

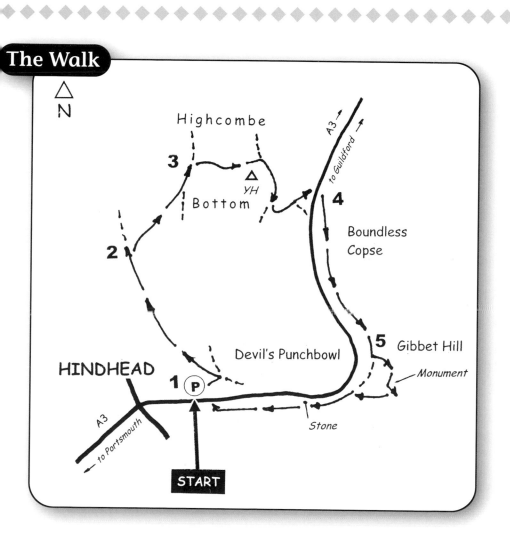

ignore a narrower path that sets off down the hillside. Soon a path joins from the left and you should keep ahead and pass the rear of gardens.

❷ When our path meets the end of a lane by an electricity sub-station, go ahead and, 10 yards before reaching a height barrier, turn right on a

1

bridleway. This lovely bridleway now descends through mature woodland to reach Highcombe Bottom 270 feet below. When the path is joined by another from the right, bear left along the well-beaten track to meet a series of field gates to left and right.

3 The circuit now leaves the bridleway and continues to the right on a narrower footpath between banks to reach a woodland brook. Cross a wooden bridge and continue ahead up a stepped path to meet a woodland track where an isolated youth hostel will be seen through the trees. Press on along the track to reach a junction with a tarmac drive. Keep ahead on the rising drive and ignore a path forking off to your right. Remain on the drive until, 30 yards before a small parking area, you should fork left on a signed footpath. Although the route is along this path to meet the A3, there is a kissing gate on your left within a few yards where a small diversion brings you to a magnificent picnic spot with stunning views. The way continues along the footpath to meet with the A3 and it is important that you resist joining

the busy road before the path finally ends.

4 Cross the A3 diagonally rightwards and continue on a wide track where you pass a National Trust sign. For some time now, this track – once the old Portsmouth road – shadows the modern A3 and it is hereabouts that the four sailors would have walked that fateful night over 200 years ago. When the track is joined by another from the right, keep ahead until on a right-hand bend a vehicle barrier is met on your left.

5 Ignore a path to your immediate left and go left passing the barrier, where you continue on a wide track to meet a junction of paths in 50 yards. Turn right here to soon meet the open hillside of Gibbet Hill some 894 feet above sea level. Pass by the granite cross that marks the site of the gibbet to reach a couple of well sited seats, another great place for a picnic. There is a toposcope on top of the trig point that will help you spot the places in the distance – enjoy the views. With the cross at your back, turn right at the trig point and soon fork right by a National Trust sign to rejoin the old Portsmouth road. Go left now and look out for a memorial stone on your right that marks the spot of the crime. Soon the A3 is reached where the National Trust café and car park brings this super circuit to an end.

DID YOU KNOW *there is a legend that says the punchbowl was created when the Devil spent his time annoying Thor, the Norse god by throwing huge handfuls of earth at him?*

◆ Background Notes ◆

On 24th September 1786, three sailors returning to their ship at Portsmouth, befriended a lone traveller also believed to be a sailor on his way to Portsmouth. As the evening closed in, they visited the Red Lion pub in Thursley for food and drink which the lone traveller paid for. Seeing that their new found friend was a man of means, the three hatched a plot to rob him and later they were all seen leaving together and disappeared into the dark night.

The next morning a shepherd found the lone traveller's lifeless body at the Devil's Punchbowl and raised the alarm. The three sailors, Edward Lonegon, James Marshall and Michael Casey were soon spotted selling the murdered man's clothes and were apprehended. After their trial at Guildford they were executed and their bodies returned to the site of the murder and hung in chains from gibbets. There the bodies swung in the breeze and decomposed for three years until, during one stormy night, their bones came crashing to the ground – a granite cross now marks the spot of the gibbet. The Red Lion is a private house nowadays, but the sailor's grave, with its miss-spelt mournful epitaph, can still be seen in St Michael's churchyard in nearby Thursley.

2

Thursley Bog and Nature Reserve

Discovering orchids, lizards and dragonflies

The bank of the Moat is great for picnicking

An interesting walk for budding naturalists that takes in a part of Thursley Bog, a rare habitat for flora and fauna. The area is managed by English Nature and is the haunt of many visiting birds and more dragonflies than you can count. Early summer brings the chance of spotting marsh orchids growing beside the path while during August tiny sand lizards can be seen basking in the sun on the boardwalks. Get down on your hands and knees and see Britain's only insect-eating plant, the tiny sundew – bring a magnifying glass. After leaving the bog the way continues along sandy paths through the drier parts of the nature reserve before returning to the scenic Moat pond, a marvellous spot where the ducks always enjoy sharing your picnic.

Thursley Bog and Nature Reserve

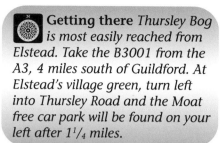 **Getting there** *Thursley Bog is most easily reached from Elstead. Take the B3001 from the A3, 4 miles south of Guildford. At Elstead's village green, turn left into Thursley Road and the Moat free car park will be found on your left after 1¹/₄ miles.*

Length of walk 2¹/₄ miles.
Time Allow 1¹/₄ hours – longer if picnicking.

Terrain Level.
Start/Parking The Moat car park (GR 899416).
Map OS Landranger 186 Aldershot & Guildford, Camberley & Haslemere.
Refreshments The Woolpack pub in Elstead is a comfortable watering hole that caters for children, who have their own menu and play area.

◆ Fun Things to See and Do ◆

During the summer months there are myriads of dragonflies patrolling the bog pools that the boardwalks lead you through. See how many different species you can spot from the viewing platform at point 1 of the walk, while at point 2 there is a fascinating identification board that will give you a better insight into these amazing creatures. The nature reserve is not only rich in dragonflies but is the haunt of many rare birds and one of the few places in the south-east where the tiny insect-eating sundew plant grows. The spoon-shaped leaves are edged in red hairs, each tipped with a sticky globule that attracts small insects. Once entrapped, the insects are slowly digested and absorbed giving the plant the much-needed nutrients that are missing in these poor acid soils. Although there are thousands of sundews here, you will need sharp eyes for they are no more than 1 cm high and 2 cm across.

Kiddiwalks in Surrey

2

1 From the car park, walk away from the road on a path that curves rightwards and shadows the bank of the Moat. Soon, at a small junction of paths, turn left to meet a sandy crossing track and an English Nature reserve sign in 30 yards. Continue ahead to meet a boardwalk. Follow the boardwalk and narrow causeway as they lead you through the famous bog. Pass by a viewing platform on your right and continue ahead between wetland pools that are constantly patrolled by dragonflies throughout summer.

2 When a boardwalk comes in from the right, turn right along it and pass under power cables to soon reach a dragonfly information board. Continue ahead through a stand of pine trees and follow the waymarked Heath Trail. When this path ends at a T-junction, ignore the Heath Trail and turn right. Go ahead at

The Walk

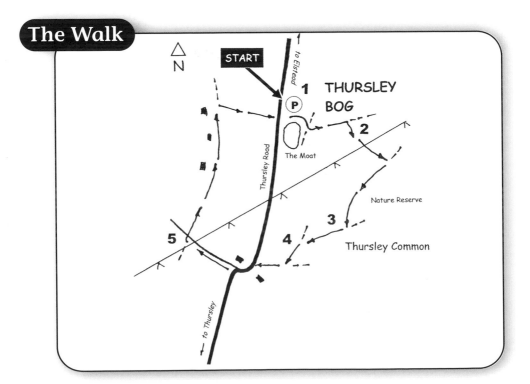

a small junction of paths by another Heath Trail post and continue until the path finally ends at another T-junction.

3 Turn right and continue on a narrow path through heather that leads you towards a large group of pine trees. Press on until the path ends at a barrier by a wide sandy bridleway.

4 Turn left along the bridleway and ignore side paths. When a large T-junction is met turn right, continue under power cables and pass through a field gate ahead and bear right to soon reach a road. Turn left alongside the road for 70 yards and as it bends sharply left, go right and immediately pass Truxford

Cottage. Press on along a narrow lane lined by MOD signs to reach a wide crossing track at the foot of a low rise.

5 Turn right at this crossing track, pass by a vehicle barrier and continue on a bridleway that leads you through very pleasant woodland. Later, as a tarmac surface is met by the garden of a house named Chailey Wood, press on ahead and pass a few select houses set well back amongst the woodland. Finally, when the ornate gateway of Elstead Manor is reached on your left, turn right and continue on a wide track through woodland to reach a road. Cross the road to enter the Moat car park to complete this super walk.

DID YOU KNOW *that dragonfly larvae live under water and breathe through gills like fish for up to five years before emerging from the water? Then, as adults, they shed their outer skin and fly off to live for only a few more months.*

◆ Background Notes ◆

The very soil that makes **Thursley Common** a great place for the naturalist has, over the centuries, saved it from the farmer and the developer. The 780-acre nature reserve is managed by English Nature and is one of the last fragments of wet heath, mire, bog pools and sphagnum lawns in southern England.

3

Compton

Counting faces on the walls

The wonderfully ornate Watts Chapel

The walk starts by one of Surrey's architectural wonders, the Watts Chapel that was built by local villagers under the guidance of Mary Watts, wife of a Victorian artist who has been described as England's Michelangelo. The chapel is in the shape of a Greek cross and wonderfully art nouveau and quite unique – even the young will be amazed at the interior. After leaving this magnificent place the route continues along the North Downs Way long-distance path. Far away from roads, this easily followed path is a delight and many wildflowers and songbirds may be seen in the hedgerows and fields. The shorter route soon begins its return to the chapel while the longer route continues through scenic fields and passes by a perfect picnic spot by a scenic lake in the grounds of Loseley Park before making its return.

Getting there *Compton is on the B3000 ¹/₂ mile east of the A3 south of Guildford. Down Lane is the first road on your left at the beginning of the village.*

Length of walk 2 or 3³/₄ miles.
Time Allow 1 hour, or 2 hours for the longer route, more if picnicking.
Terrain Gently undulating.
Start/parking Small parking area by the Watts Chapel in Down Lane (GR 967474).
Map OS Landranger 186 Aldershot & Guildford, Camberley & Haslemere.
Refreshments Near the beginning of the walk the route passes the Watts Gallery where a teashop is open from 10.30 am until 5.30 pm each day.

❶ From the parking area, walk along Down Lane away from the B3000 and pass Coneycroft Farm. Continue along the lane until you meet with a North Downs Way sign on your right. Our way is right along the North Downs Way on a sandy track. After passing between farm buildings the track narrows and rises to meet with a junction of paths.

❷ *The shorter circuit now turns right downhill between banks to meet some steps on the right. You then continue from point 5 below.*

◆ Fun Things to See and Do ◆

There are many faces painted and sculpted both on the inside and outside of the Watts Chapel and all are unique. Admire the sheer skill of the villagers who created this magnificent place. I tried to count the number of faces but found it an almost impossible task and after finding 70 on the inside and 55 on the outside I became totally confused. See how you get on, but be warned it is no easy task.

Detail from the Watts Chapel

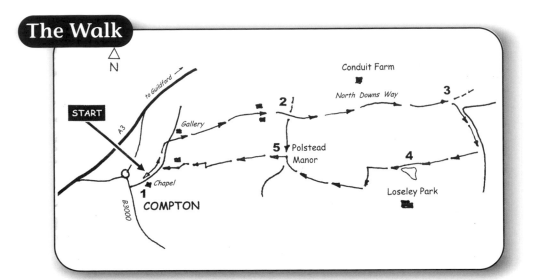

The longer circuit continues ahead at this junction and enters woodland where there are occasional glimpses of the Hogs Back that the path shadows. As you exit the woodland you will see power cables 30 yards ahead of you. Ignore a path on your right, and press on under the cables to reach a T-junction with a farm track in 80 yards. Continue right along the track that now gives fine views over fields to your left. After continuing through more woodland, a stile and gate are met with a T-junction and a track beyond.

❸ We now leave the North Downs Way long-distance path as our way turns right to meet a junction of country lanes in 80 yards. Fork right down Littleton Lane watching out for the occasional motorist and, when a road junction is met, turn right on a public footpath to reach a stile. Enter a field and press on ahead through a second to finally cross a stile and find yourself by a lake and picnic spot.

❹ The circuit continues alongside the lake edge to a stile where you go ahead along a field edge. After crossing two stiles in quick succession turn left in 50 yards

◆ ◆

and continue alongside the grounds of Loseley House to reach a driveway. Turn right and remain on the drive until it meets with a lane by a group of houses. Turn right here on a narrow path to meet with steps in the left bank in 50 yards.

5 *Both circuits continue from this point.*

Climb the steps and continue on a fenced path that skirts a large garden to reach a stile where you enter a field and continue ahead along the right-hand edge. At a stile turn right to meet a concrete farm drive and soon pass to the left of a large barn. Follow the arrows left and soon meet Downs Lane where a few yards to your left is the Watts Chapel and the end of this good walk.

DID YOU KNOW *that the old wives' tale saying that picking dandelions causes bed-wetting is partially true? Dandelion is a diuretic and for centuries was used as a medicine to treat dropsy (heart disease) by preventing the body from retaining water.*

◆ Background Notes ◆

Mary Watts was a talented young potter who believed passionately in the *Home Arts and Industries Association* that had been set up in 1885 to encourage the lower classes to take an interest in handicrafts in the hope of keeping them out of the gin houses. She was married to George Frederick Watts, an important Victorian painter, and they lived at Limnerslease a little further along the lane from the Watt's Gallery.

When the old graveyard in the village became full to capacity, Mary wrote to the council with a proposal to build a new cemetery and chapel. She sent them a clay model of the chapel in 1895 and, after its approval, land was purchased for the site. The exterior of the chapel was completed in 1898 and the interior in 1904, the year of George's death.

4
Pirbright

Dr Livingstone, I presume?

The scenic pond at the Fox Corner Wildlife Area

Everyone must have heard of Stanley trekking through the jungles of darkest Africa for month after month in his search for the missionary and explorer, Dr David Livingstone – well this great circuit passes Stanley's last resting place and, although not as taxing as Stanley's adventure, this lovely route through fields and woodland allows children to do some exploring themselves. The halfway point of the circuit is reached at the Fox Corner Wildlife Area, a wonderful place where children can make their own discoveries. A little further into the reserve brings you to a scenic pond just brimming with aquatic life and a great picnic spot. The return journey passes through lovely woodland and passes 16th-century White's Farm before rejoining Pirbright's large village green which itself is a good place for a picnic.

Getting there *Pirbright is on the A324, 4 miles north of Guildford. When travelling from the Guildford direction, turn right beside the White Hart pub and a lay-by will be met in 150 yards on your left. There is further parking around the green.*

Length of walk 4 miles.
Time Allow 2 hours, more if picnicking.

Terrain Level.
Start/parking The lay-by beside the pond on Pirbright's village green (GR 947559).
Map OS Landranger 186 Aldershot & Guildford, Camberley & Haslemere.
Refreshments The White Hart and the Cricketers pubs are both on the route.

◆ Fun Things to See and Do ◆

 The halfway point of the walk is at the Fox Corner Wildlife Area which is a fantastic place to see birds, butterflies, dragonflies and aquatic life. There are a couple of informative boards that will help you – see how many of these things you can identify.

The circuit passes through lovely woodland – can you spot and name these trees from their bark – the clues may help?

A. Not gold but ...   B. From the top of Britain.   C. Nelson's ship was built of this.

Answers at the end of this walk.

Kiddiwalks in Surrey

4

1 From the pond, walk back to the A324 besides the White Hart pub and cross the main road diagonally right passing by Hatchers, a 16th-century cottage. When a small lane is soon met, go left along it and just before a right bend you will see Stanley's grave marked by a granite monolith to your right. Press on along the lane and turn right over a stream immediately after passing St Michael's church.

2 Now follow a well-trodden path between fields to reach a road. Here turn right and continue along the road until it ends at traffic lights. Cross the road and continue along a tarmac drive that bears off to the left. When Holly Lodge is reached, turn right on a bridleway and soon pass over three brooks to reach a road. Press on ahead along the marked bridleway to meet a quiet residential road.

The Walk

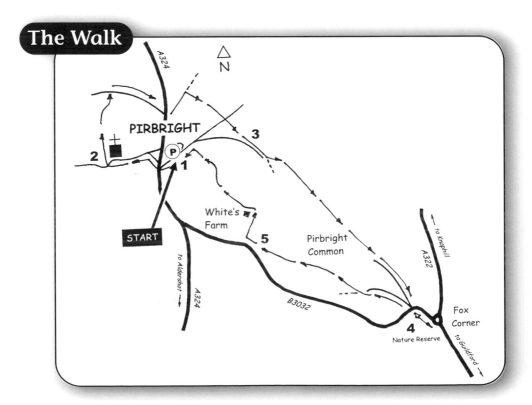

3 Fork left here and remain alongside the road until, 130 yards after it ends, fork left on a signed public byway. Remain on this wide track as it leads you easily across Pirbright Common. The track eventually meets a few well-spaced houses before reaching a road junction at Fox Corner. Go ahead alongside the road and in 180 yards go right into the Fox Corner Wildlife Area – the halfway point of the circuit and a wonderful place for youngsters to explore. A surfaced path soon brings you to a scenic pond and a great site for a picnic.

4 The return to Pirbright begins by retracing your steps back to the road junction by the byway where you now follow a signed footpath along Heath Mill Lane. Look out for Heath Mill, now a house but still with the remains of its waterwheel. After 70 yards, fork right to a directional post and ignore a footpath heading off left. Keep ahead now on the wide path and ignore side paths. When a small lane is reached, go ahead and soon continue along a fenced path behind gardens until it ends by a little-used road.

5 Continue ahead to meet White's Lane after 80 yards and

Sir Stanley's gravestone

turn right along it. Immediately after passing 16th-century White's Farm, turn left on a narrow path to meet and cross a stile and then go left across a small meadow. Cross a stile and enter woodland where you follow a well-trodden path between the trees. The path brings you to a plant nursery (overgrown at the time of writing), where you continue past greenhouses before turning left along a drive and passing through a gate. Press on ahead to very soon meet with the village green besides the Cricketers pub. This great circuit ends just a few yards to your left by the village pond.

Kiddiwalks in Surrey

4

DID YOU KNOW *that Stanley's wish was to be buried beside Livingstone in Westminster Abbey but this was denied him?*

◆ Background Notes ◆

Sir Henry Morton Stanley was born in 1841, the illegitimate son of John Rowlands and brought up in a workhouse. At the age of 18 he sailed to New Orleans as a cabin boy and there was employed and befriended by Henry Stanley, whose name he took. After fighting in the American Civil War he became a special correspondent for *The New York Herald* and two years later was commissioned to travel to Africa and cover the search for the explorer Dr David Livingstone, of whom nothing had been heard for almost two years since he set off in search of the source of the Nile.

An epic journey through dense jungle ensued before he discovered Livingstone at Ujiji in November 1872 and greeted him with his famous words 'Dr Livingstone, I presume?' After Livingstone's death in 1873, Stanley continued exploring Africa and returned to Britain in 1890 when he married. By 1895 he was elected MP for North Lambeth and received his knighthood in 1899. He spent his last years at his home in Pirbright and died in 1904.

Answers.   A. Silver Birch   B. Scots Pine   C. Oak

5

Chobham Common

In the footsteps of Queen Victoria

The wide paths across the common are easy to follow

In 1853 Queen Victoria reviewed 8,000 of her troops on Chobham Common, a colourful event unusual enough to be marked by a monument in the form of a Runic cross paid for by appreciative locals and erected in 1901. Imagine the sights and sounds of 8,000 soldiers massed here dressed in their bright red tunics, with their highly polished boots gleaming in the sun. The circuit starts beside the cross and continues through a nature reserve that is full of interest. There is a chance to discover rare plants and, if you are quiet, you may spot a roe deer. Wide sandy paths across the undulating common are easy to follow and offer lovely views over the swathes of heather. Along the way there are plenty of pretty picnic spots with fine views.

Getting there *Chobham Common is 3 miles north of Chobham. Travel north from Chobham along the B383 Windsor Road for 2¹/₂ miles and cross the M3. Continue ahead at a roundabout where you ignore a car park. A further ¹/₄ mile brings you to the Monument car park on your right.*

Length of walk 2¹/₄ miles.
Time Allow 1¹/₂ hours, more if picnicking.
Terrain Gently undulating – suitable for buggies and pushchairs.
Start/parking The Monument car park on Chobham Common (GR 965654).
Map OS Landranger 176 West London area.
Refreshments There is a range of eateries in Chobham.

❶ From the car park pass by a vehicle barrier and continue on a rising path where you will see the monument to your left. Press on at the crest of the rise to meet a junction of paths. Continue ahead and soon there are great

◆ Fun Things to See and Do ◆

Make an interesting plaque by collecting a few stems of grass that have prominent seed heads. When you get home, cover a flat surface with greaseproof paper and roll out a piece of children's modelling dough in an oblong shape to about 5mm thick. Now lay the grass on the dough; either use a single stem as I have done or an attractive group and then very carefully roller them in. Now lift the grass from the dough to see your design. For a permanent sculpture use Das modelling clay which air-dries and hardens in two days. Make a small hole in the top with a pencil before it dries so that you can hang your plaque on a wall. See walk 19 for a different type of sculpture, or why not try an idea of your own.

views across the common towards Sunningdale. This lovely path now crosses Ship Hill where the predominant plant is heather, dotted with birch, but look out for the stunning clumps of grass that line the way.

The Walk

2 As the path nears a railway line ahead, continue on it as it bears off to the right and ignore a right fork. The path soon passes through a shallow depression where there is a small heathland pool that brings refreshment to the mammals that live here and is frequented by damselflies and dragonflies. You may also see the common centaury growing along the drier parts of this path – it is named after one of the Centaurs of Greek mythology who reputedly used it as a medicine. Ignore a right fork and soon at a junction of paths bear left on the main path. Eventually a vehicle barrier comes into view.

3 Turn right 10 yards before this barrier onto a bridleway and, at a junction of paths, turn right on another bridleway. Now ignore all side paths and remain on this wide bridleway as it crosses the open expanse of the common and finally ends at a T-junction by a seat and a marker post.

❹ Turn right and after 80 yards, at a junction of paths, turn right and continue ahead on a gently rising path that brings you to a car park. Go right along the face of the car park and cross a picnic meadow on a path that passes through birch woodland. When the open heath is reached, press on ahead to reach a T-junction. Turn left now along the wide stony track and, when at the top of a rise by a marker post, turn left and soon pass by the Runic cross to return to the car park.

DID YOU KNOW *that the encampment on the common of so large a body of men for the Queen's review brought calls for a permanent camp to be built in the area? Within a couple of years the military town of Aldershot came into being.*

◆ Background Notes ◆

Chobham Common is an ancient landscape that was created by prehistoric farmers as they cleared the woodland for cultivation. With the loss of their covering, the light sandy soils soon began to deteriorate to become the acid soil that heather and gorse thrive on. Unfortunately, birch also enjoys this environment and, since the grazing of cattle ceased on the common a century ago, Surrey County Council has been forced to stem the growth of the birch in order to maintain the heathland habitat.

The common is an SSSI and is the best site in Britain to see rare ants, wasps, bees and aquatic beetles. Wild flowers such as marsh gentian and southern marsh orchid are found here, as well as many birds, including the Dartford warbler, nightjar, stonechat and the rare hobby.

6

Cooper's Hill

Climb the steps of the 'control tower'

The Runnymede Pleasure Grounds

This walk starts from the unique Commonwealth Air Forces Memorial that sits atop Cooper's Hill. The memorial resembles an airfield control tower and commemorates those airmen and women from the Second World War who have no known grave. Although it is a solemn place and is to be treated with respect, children will love to climb the series of circular steps to reach a viewing gallery where a final climb brings you to the roof, with its commanding views over the river Thames. The circuit continues down the magnificent wooded slopes of Cooper's Hill to the world famous water meadows of Runnymede and for a short while follows the bank of the Thames. The return route is through beautiful wildflower meadows and past Langham's Pond, an SSSI, before rejoining the serene woodland of Cooper's Hill and the climb back to the Airmen's Memorial.

Kiddiwalks in Surrey

6 ◆◆◆◆◆◆◆◆◆◆◆◆◆◆◆◆◆◆◆◆◆◆◆◆◆◆◆◆

Getting there The Commonwealth Air Forces Memorial is signposted from the A30, just south of Egham. Follow the signs west along the A328.

Length of walk 3 miles.

Time Allow 2 hours.

Terrain The circuit rises by 200 feet on a not-too-difficult path towards its end.

Start/parking The free car park by the Commonwealth Airmen's Memorial (GR 996718).

Map OS Landranger 176 West London Area.

Refreshments The circuit passes through the Runnymede Pleasure Grounds where the Runnymede Cafeteria offers a good selection of simple hot and cold snacks, as well as a wide variety of ice creams.

1 From the car park turn right along the lane to reach the memorial. This is a not-to-be-missed experience, so take your time to explore. After your visit, return to the memorial gates, turn left along the lane and remain on the lane until you meet a kissing gate on your left. Go left through it and continue downhill on the well-trodden path that leads you through the splendours of Cooper's Hill oak woodland.

2 When finally at the foot of the slope, continue on through kissing gates to reach the famous water meadows where you should remain ahead to meet and cross the A308. Now turn right on a distinct grassy path that follows the bank of the Thames. When the path swings left, you will

◆ Fun Things to See and Do ◆

Bring a pair of binoculars with you as there are fantastic views from the Commonwealth Airmen's Memorial Tower, of Windsor Castle, sailing boats on a reservoir, motor boats on the Thames, and airliners taking off from Heathrow airport. Binoculars will also help you spot the interesting wildlife on Langham's Pond that is passed on the second half of the circuit.

The Walk

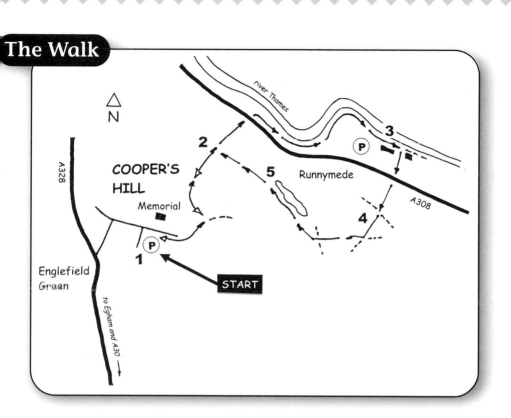

meet the large open grassy area of the Runnymede Pleasure Grounds.

❸ The route continues along the riverbank and, as it leaves the Pleasure Grounds behind, it passes a few well-sited houses that enjoy scenic river views. Immediately after passing a rather ugly commercial building, turn right between it and Thames Cottage to soon meet

the A308 which you cross to a stile opposite. Now press on ahead along a footpath numbered 14 that leads you through a magnificent wild flower meadow.

❹ Remain ahead at a crossing path and keep a hedgerow on your right. As the hedgerow bends away to the right, another crossing path is met and here you should turn right along it.

Some 60 yards before reaching a hedgerow ahead of you, turn right again on a well defined path. Ignore a boarded walkway on your right and press on ahead through a kissing gate and bear right along the edge of Langham's Pond, a Site of Special Scientific Interest. Press on along the waters' edge to finally cross a stile in a hedgerow ahead of you.

5 Continue on a short boarded walkway to rejoin the open water meadow where you should now turn left alongside a wire fence to reach a directional post ahead. At the post turn left and retrace your steps up the slopes of Cooper's Hill to rejoin the Memorial and the car park beyond.

DID YOU KNOW *that the name Magna Carta is Latin for Great Charter?*

◆ **Background Notes** ◆

Runnymede holds a special place in English history, as it is the place that common law and justice was born. Back in June of 1215, after a bitter and long-running dispute over money and taxes with his powerful barons, King John was forced to sign away most of his power in a document known as Magna Carta.

Archbishop Langdon brokered the meeting and both parties came together in the water meadows of Runnymede. The document, which contained 63 clauses, was presented to the king for him to sign and so was born our liberty and freedom. It is by far the most important document of medieval England and its clauses have become entrenched in constitutions around the world. Interestingly, the shortest, and possibly the most effective clause reads 'To none will we sell, to none deny or delay, right of justice'.

7

Hascombe

Discovering an ancient hill fort

A family of Canada geese enjoy the waters of Hascombe village pond

This wonderful circuit passes a scenic pond and idyllic cottages in Hascombe village before climbing to the top of Hascombe Hill and discovering an Iron Age hill fort some 260 feet above. Older children will enjoy the challenge of the climb and all ages will be rewarded by the breathtaking views. The easily followed path then continues along the top of the ridge through the dappled shade of indigenous woodland where occasional keyhole views across the Surrey landscape are seen. The way returns on a wonderful downhill path beside ploughlands where there are views across the village in the valley below. Bring a picnic with you as the return route re-passes the village pond where handily placed seats make it such a welcoming spot to relax.

Kiddiwalks in Surrey

 Getting there *Take the B2130 south-east from Godalming to meet Hascombe in 3¹/₂ miles. Look out for Mare Lane on your right signed to the village hall. Park alongside Mare Lane.*

Length of walk 3 miles.
Time Allow 1¹/₂ hours.
Terrain One long, but not difficult, hill that climbs 260 feet in the first mile.
Start/parking Mare Lane (GR 997398).
Map OS Landranger 186 Aldershot & Guildford, Camberley & Haslemere.
Refreshments The White Horse pub is passed along the route and caters for all ages.

1 From Mare Lane walk back to the B2130 and turn right for a few yards to meet a wonderful spring that offers great drinking water for man and beast. Cross directly over the road and continue on a path alongside Fountain Cottage. Soon cross a stream and press on ahead when a bridleway is met.

2 When pretty Lower House is reached, turn right along a quiet driveway with a field to your right where rabbits are often seen grazing amongst the horses. Soon pass the village pond and a couple of pretty cottages to meet with the White Horse public house. Pass the front of the pub and then turn immediately left

◆ Fun Things to See and Do ◆

 For almost the entire way, the route is far away from roads so children will be free to explore the wonderful countryside this circuit offers. Bring a field guide to help in identifying the many wildflowers, birds and mammals to be seen along the route. Some of the things you can expect to see during the summer months are red campion, foxgloves, herb Robert, damselflies, water birds, squirrels, rabbits, pheasants and deer.

The Walk

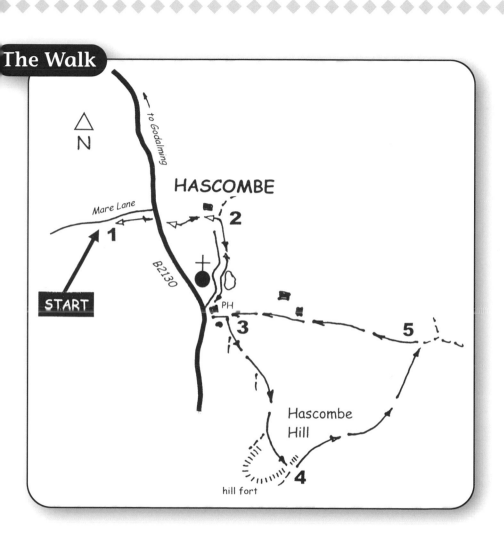

on a bridleway that runs along a driveway. After 200 yards the entrance to Hascombe Place Farm House is reached and here you should turn right on a signposted footpath that begins beside a brick built garage.

3 Press on ahead as the deeply eroded path climbs between banks and, when the garage is just out of site, a fork is met. Bear left here and keep ahead when another path from the right joins our way. The flora begins to change now and, during summer, foxgloves will be seen lining the path. A plant that looks pretty here but is unwanted is the rhododendron, a rather invasive foreigner. Keep left at a fork that divides to pass a large beech tree and when the path begins to level and becomes grassier, keep right at a fork. Pass between two huge fir trees to reach a seat hewn out of a tree trunk. Continue to the right of this seat to discover our goal, one of the highest and best views in Surrey. The earthworks of the hill fort are on your right should you wish to explore them.

4 With the climb now over, press on down a short slope to meet a crossing path and turn left. The way enters woodland and follows the line of the ridge where you will see keyhole views across the countryside. Ignore all side paths and remain ahead on the well-trodden path as it follows the ridge. Along the way Victorian railings will be seen embedded in a couple of trees that have grown around them.

5 After going downhill between trees and passing through posts a crossing path is met. Turn left along this pretty path that will lead you into the valley below beside a wide field where the quiet walker may be rewarded by the sight of wild deer grazing on

View from the Iron Age hill fort

the opposite field edge. After passing by a farm cottage, continue ahead along a driveway that brings you directly back to the White Horse pub where, by turning right along the lane, you pass the village pond again. Now retrace your footsteps, remembering to fork left onto the narrower path that brings you back to the village spring. A word of warning here – keep children in close check now as the path ends very abruptly at the roadside!

DID YOU KNOW *that the oak tree provides more food and shelter for our wildlife than any other tree? Insects and small animals eat its roots, bark, fruit and leaves and they, in turn, are eaten by birds and animals like dormice and wood mice – in all about 300 different species receive nourishment from the oak.*

◆ Background Notes ◆

Dating from around 700 BC, **Hascombe Hill's Iron Age fort** can still be made out as it follows the contours of the hilltop. The earthwork would have been interlaced with tree boughs and stones to increase its height and was undoubtedly constructed and manned by a warrior elite within iron-age society. It provided a stronghold against other tribes in times of unrest while during peacetime it would probably have served as an administrative centre and a place for their feasts.

The fort had commanding 360-degree views over the surrounding countryside, which would allow time for the local tribe to take up defensive positions when necessary. As peaceful times came, the hill was abandoned and the more comfortable valley below became populated although the village of Hascombe remained quite remote and cut off from the rest of Surrey right up to the beginning of the 19th century. Before Hascombe Hill became heavily forested, John Aubrey, an 18th-century chronicler of Surrey, remarked that the bare hilltop was *'a convenient place to make a map'*.

8

Chilworth

Gunpowder, one of man's damnable inventions

This shallow leat is great for safe paddling

A lovely walk that starts in peaceful woodland where only bird song and the sound of running water breaks the silence. Amongst the trees will be found the stark remains of Chilworth's old gunpowder mills, at one time the most important in England. Just imagine the scene as horses pulled wagons along wooden tramways, water rushed down leats to power the mills and 400 workers went about the business of making their deadly product. Youngsters will enjoy the challenge of climbing to St Martha's church, high on the hill above, where the views are outstanding. The descent brings you to Chilworth Manor below where the way soon rejoins the woodland and the cool waters of the Tilling Bourne – bring a picnic.

Chilworth

Getting there *Chilworth is south of Guildford on the A248 between Shalford and Albury.*

Length of walk 3 miles.
Time Allow 2 hours, more if picnicking.
Terrain Level apart from one stiff climb of 390 feet to St Martha's

church and a fairly steep descent from it.
Start/parking The A248 roadside by Chilworth Infants School (GR 029473).
Map OS Landranger 186 Aldershot & Guildford, Camberley & Haslemere.
Refreshments The Percy Arms is at the beginning of the walk and serves a variety of food.

❶ Follow a narrow path to the left of the infant school to reach a wooden bridge over a leat. The path follows the course of a tramway where horses once pulled their loads of gunpowder to the railway in Chilworth and on your right by the bridge is a remaining part. Fork right and soon turn right and pass picnic tables in a clearing. Keep to the wide path through woodland and ignore a left fork by a mound of earth. Soon pass by the remains of the mill buildings to reach an information board and a bridge.

❷ Turn right over the bridge and cross a stile ahead of you to enter a field. Press on through a second

---

◆ Fun Things to See and Do ◆

An attraction for children here is a shallow leat that is great for safe paddling while a large fallen tree trunk offers the brave an opportunity of crossing the shallow water without getting their feet wet. Older children will enjoy the challenge of reaching St Martha's church, high on the hill above the stream.

The Walk

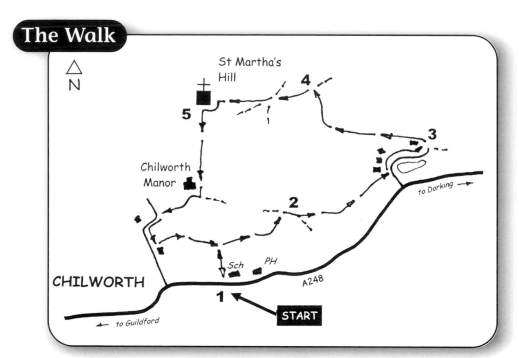

and third field with more recent evidence of the gunpowder works through the trees on your left. After the path narrows and passes the rear of gardens, a road is met. Bear left over a bridge and continue along a tarmac drive with housing on your left and a lake to your right. This was the site of Postford Mill, originally a paper mill before changing to a flock mill. After its closure it became a fish farm before finally succumbing to housing. Continue along the drive and, when it bends sharply left, ignore a footpath ahead of you.

❸ At the gateway to Millstream Cottage ignore a path on the right and fork left alongside the garden. Soon you are immersed in majestic beech woodland where you gradually gain height and leave the Tilling Bourne flowing between the trees below you before the path bends away from the stream and begins the climb in earnest. When an undulating field is seen to your left, keep right on the main path and when nearing the top of the hill ignore a right fork. Soon reach a directional post by a clearing that is the haunt of green woodpeckers that feed on the anthills here.

A real of sense of achievement is felt when you reach St Martha's

④ Turn left along the rising sandy bridleway and keep ahead in 50 yards at a junction of tracks. Pass by a Second World War pillbox and keep to the bridleway as you pass by a Downs Link path on your left. When the track divides, leave the bridleway and go ahead on a public footpath that will finally bring you to St Martha's church and the end of the climb. Continue left around the wall of the graveyard to find welcoming seats that offer stunning views and a good excuse to rest awhile. Just the other side of the wall is the grave of one of the Second World War's most charismatic leaders, Major General Bernard Freyberg VC who, although being English, commanded New Zealand troops. A little further away is the grave of Sir George Edwards, a man who had his hand in many aircraft designs and later, as chairman of the British Aircraft Corporation, ensured that Concorde entered into service.

⑤ The return to the valley below begins on a downhill path directly in front of the seats. The path is steep and caution should be used. Remain on the path until it ends at a T-junction with a field beyond. Turn right to join

Kiddiwalks in Surrey

the drive of Chilworth Manor and follow it leftwards to reach a road. Continue ahead along the road and after it passes over a second bridge turn immediately left on a path by a lodge gate that was once the entrance to the gunpowder mills. Continue ahead on the wide path where again you will detect the remains of the mills in the woodland. Finally cross a bridge over the leat on your right to rejoin the infant school and the end of this great circuit.

DID YOU KNOW *that the leaves of the stinging nettle are covered in tiny brittle hollow hairs containing formic acid? When broken they eject their contents onto your skin causing an instantly painful rash. The dead nettle is so named because it has no sting.*

◆ Background Notes ◆

Mills have occupied the Chilworth site since Domesday although they were most likely corn mills. Gunpowder came to Chilworth as early as 1580 and, by 1625, the East India Company operated them. Water provided the power source during the early days but in 1885, when the Chilworth Gunpowder Company was formed, power came from a stationary engine. During the 1890s, and the development of 'high explosives', the site expanded over the fields westward.

Originally the gunpowder was carried by punt along the Tilling Bourne to the river Wey at Shalford where it was loaded onto barges for its journey to London. At the coming of the railway to Chilworth in 1888, the works' internal railway, operated by horse drawn wagons, was extended to Chilworth station. Two years after the end of the First World War, the works became a part of Noble Industries but soon closed and Noble was later swallowed up by ICI.

New Haw

Victorian watermill and canal bank

Weybridge Town Lock

This circuit starts beside New Haw Lock on the Wey Navigation and is surprisingly rural for a route that is so penned in by the housing and industry of Weybridge, Addlestone and Byfleet. It begins by following a path beside fields to reach a track that brings you to a short picturesque section of the river Wey. After crossing a railway line the route follows a quiet lane that shadows the river and brings you to the halfway point at Weybridge Town Lock where colourful narrow boats negotiate the lock gates. Following the towpath from here brings you to Coxes Lock and Mill, another fascinating spot where a grassy area makes an interesting picnic spot with good views of the boats as they enter and leave the lock. Continuing along the towpath, where idyllic gardens tumble down to the waters' edge, brings you back to New Haw Lock and the end of this appealing walk.

9

Getting there *New Haw is 1³/₄ miles west of Weybridge on the A318 between Brooklands and Addlestone.*

Length of walk 3¹/₄ miles.
Time Allow 2 hours, more if picnicking.
Terrain Level – suitable for buggies and pushchairs.
Start/parking The parking area is off the A318, 100 yards

south-east of the New Haw roundabout (GR 055630).
Map OS Landranger 187 Dorking & Reigate, Crawley & Horsham.
Refreshments These can be found at the White Hart pub just the other side of the New Haw roundabout.

◆ Fun Things to See and Do ◆

Compare the difference between the natural river Wey seen near the beginning of the walk and the Wey Navigation seen later. Whereas the river is only suitable for fishing, the canal provided enough water for the barges to ply their trade. There is a drop of 68 feet between Guildford and Weybridge that the canal overcomes by the use of 12 locks. Watch how the lock gates work and how easily the narrow boats are raised to the next level, but be careful to stay away from the edge.

The Walk

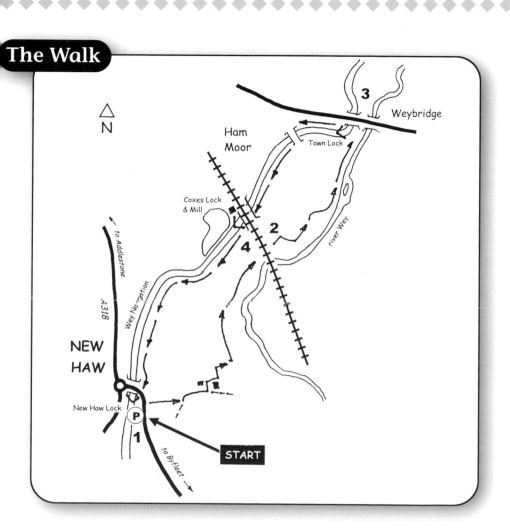

1 Go back to the entrance of the parking area and cross the A318 diagonally left to meet a public footpath. Continue along this path as it passes gardens to reach a drive. Turn left along the drive and remain on it as it bends sharply left by Wey Manor Farm. Keep to a track now as it zigzags beside fields. Ignore the occasional side path and remain on the track until a height barrier

A narrow boat leaves Coxes Lock with the mill in the background

is reached. Turn right here on a signed footpath and pass under a second height barrier to reach the bank of the picturesque river Wey. The path shadows the bank for a short distance before swinging left and skirting the grounds of the Wey Island Trust to soon meet the end of the track. Youngsters should now be kept in close check as you cross a stile and go ahead to reach an unfenced railway line. Please take good note of the Stop Look and Listen sign before crossing the rails.

2 At the far side bear left on a driveway that passes the side of

park homes and soon fork right along the drive to reach a quiet lane. Press on now along the lane where there is a strange mixture of small shacks almost lost to undergrowth and large salubrious houses. Parts of the river Wey will again be seen on your right and the lane finally ends at Weybridge Town Lock.

3 Now cross the road and go left along the pavement and cross a bridge. Some 50 yards later re-cross the road to meet the towpath and press on along a short section of towpath to reach a small vehicle bridge. (The towpath is narrow here so if you are pushing a buggy you may choose to stay on the pavement beside the road until the small vehicle bridge is seen on your left.) Go left over the bridge and now continue along the left-hand towpath until you reach Coxes Lock with the converted buildings of the mill on the far bank – it's a great spot to sit and watch the narrow boats.

❹ Continue along the left-hand towpath to eventually reach a road bridge a few yards before New Haw Lock. Go up to the road which you cross to the parking area opposite where this interesting circuit ends.

DID YOU KNOW *that Weybridge is named after the river Wey that meets with the river Thames just $^1/_2$ mile north of Weybridge Town Lock?*

◆ Background Notes ◆

The River Wey Navigation was one of the first canals to be built in Britain and was designed and built in 1651 by Sir Richard Weston. He inserted lock gates, one of which has a rise of only a few inches, and 'canalised' parts of the meandering river making it possible for river traffic to reach Guildford from the river Thames.

Coxes Mill was built in 1777 and its huge millpond was designed so as not to interrupt the flow of water from the canal. After serving originally as a steel mill it later converted to corn milling and for a short time to a silk mill. A massive silo was added between 1901 and 1906 and grain milling continued until 1969, with 70-foot barges bringing their cargoes from Tilbury. A short revival came in 1981 when barge traffic restarted and proved a 70% fuel saving over the equivalent road haulage but this only lasted for a couple of years before the mill finally closed. The building now sees life as an exclusive housing complex where apartments have balconies with enviable views over the waterway.

10
Sidney Wood

Discovering London's lost route to the sea

This is a great walk through beautiful Sidney Wood that, over the years, has done its best to reclaim the Wey & Arun Canal since its closure in 1871. The canal, one of Britain's last and possibly least profitable canals, was built to link the Wey Navigation and the river Arun, thereby giving access to the south coast for barges from London. This level circuit is through some of the best indigenous woodland Surrey can offer and amongst the trees we discover parts of the defunct canal. With only tuneful birdsong breaking the quietness of the woodland, and being far away from roads, it is an ideal place for youngsters to explore and let off steam. Sidney Wood is a great picnic spot as well as being a fantastic area for budding naturalists.

Sidney Wood

Getting there *Sidney Wood is 1 mile west of the A281 on a country lane that links Alfold Crossways to Dunsfold.*

Length of walk 2³/₄ miles.
Time Allow 1¹/₂ hours.
Terrain Level – suitable for pushchairs and buggies. Some parts may become muddy during winter.

Start/parking Sidney Wood car park (GR 026351).
Map OS Landranger 186 Aldershot & Guildford, Camberley & Haslemere.
Refreshments The closest refreshment places are the Sun Inn at Dunsfold and the Crown pub in Alfold.

◆ Fun Things to See and Do ◆

The entire walk is away from roads, so children can explore the woodland to their hearts' content. When you discover the old canal – now not much more than an indentation in the woodland – try to imagine what it would have been like here some 150 years ago as horses toiled along the towpath with their water-borne loads in tow. The sights and sounds in this now peaceful woodland would have been rather different then.

A useful addition to take with you would be a field guide to help children identify the many birds that will be seen and heard along the way. June is the best time to see the common spotted orchids that line much of the route.

The common spotted orchid

10

❶ From the car park walk back to the track that led you here and turn rightwards along it with your back to the road. The track ends at a T-junction. Turn right along the broad track where, during early-summer, orchids flower in the margins.

❷ At a junction of tracks by an equestrian centre to your right, go ahead on a narrower path that continues between trees. Ignore side paths and remain on the main path and it is not long before *London's lost route to the sea* is discovered beneath the trees.

❸ Go over the canal and turn immediately left along its restored towpath. Soon pass a concrete marker post that informs you that the river Arun is 13 miles ahead while the river Wey is 10 miles behind you. As you press on along the towpath you can see

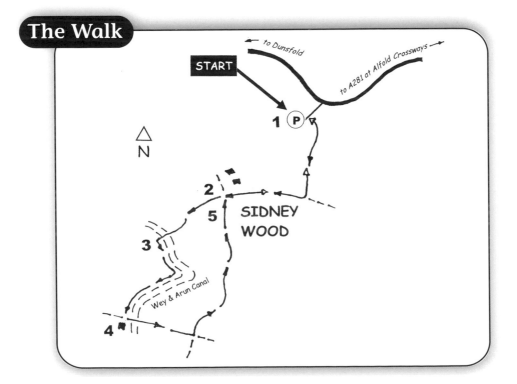

how volunteers from the Wey & Arun Canal Trust have improved this part of the mainly waterless canal, while later an unrestored section illustrates just how, left to their own devices, the trees take over.

4 At a junction of tracks with a house beyond, turn left along a forest track. Ignore a drive to an unseen house on your right and press on through a vehicle barrier. At another junction of wide tracks turn left. Now continue along this wide sunny track until the junction of tracks by the equestrian centre is met.

5 Turn right here and retrace your steps back to the car park.

DID YOU KNOW *that mushrooms and toadstools are only the fruiting body of the plant, just as an apple is on a tree? The main part, called mycelium consists of very fine threads buried underground or within a tree.*

◆ Background Notes ◆

The plans for the Wey and Arun Canal were conceived during the Napoleonic wars when French warships threatened our seaborne supply route from London around the Kent and Sussex coast to the battle fleet in Portsmouth. The canal was built to link the river Thames to Portsmouth via the Wey Navigation, the Wey and Arun Canal, the Arun Navigation and finally the Portsmouth and Arundel canal, making it an important military canal route.

However, after Napoleon's defeat, the seaward journey again became viable and, for a while, the Wey and Arun Canal continued to play a useful role transporting agricultural produce, coal and building materials until increased competition from the railways and improved roads to the coast finally sealed its fate. Now known as '*London's lost route to the sea*', it is largely in a state of disrepair with many sections completely levelled. Sterling efforts from members of the Wey & Arun Canal Trust must be applauded for their attempts to restore parts of this largely forgotten waterway.

11
Shere

The jewel in Surrey's crown

Lower Street with the old jail in the background

This walk is around one of Surrey's prettiest villages where centuries-old cottages line the narrow streets. Cutting through the centre of the village are the clear waters of the Tilling Bourne stream, a favourite with children who enjoy paddling in the cool waters and feeding the resident ducks. Using village lanes, the circuit starts its tour and soon passes an old house that served as the village prison 300 years ago. After shadowing the bank of the Tilling Bourne through a field for a short distance, and maybe enjoying a paddle in the stream, the way turns south to reach rising ground where there are fine views over the fields towards the North Downs. Continuing along a couple of quiet streets to reach a field, the way soon turns and takes you to St James's church where the Tilling Bourne is crossed to reach a quaint village street which completes the circuit.

◆ ◆

 Getting there *Shere is signed off the A25, 6 miles west of Dorking.*

Length of walk 1¹/₂ miles.
Time Allow 1 hour.
Terrain Fairly level – suitable for buggies and pushchairs.
Start/parking The small car park by the recreation ground next to the Manor House in Upper Street or at the roadside in Gomshall Lane (car park GR 073480; roadside GR 075479).
Map OS Landranger 187 Dorking & Reigate, Crawley & Horsham.
Refreshments The Lucky Duck tearooms in Middle Street offer olde worlde charm as well as drinks, sandwiches and cakes.

❶ From the car park turn left to meet Middle Street or, if you have parked in Gomshall Lane, walk west to Middle Street. Continue along Middle Street where you pass by what was once the village fire station but is now a striking public convenience. Cross the Tilling Bourne and turn right into Lower Street. Press on along Lower Street where you soon pass the Old Forge followed by the Old Prison – both now making very comfortable cottages. Keep ahead, with very well tended allotments on your right.

❷ When the road ends, ignore a ford on your right and continue along a track to reach a kissing gate. Pass through the gate and follow the water's edge to another kissing gate. An ingenious roofed seat will be seen ahead of you that

◆ Fun Things to See and Do ◆

 Bring some bread with you as the resident ducks are generally found at the water's edge alongside Lower Street and eagerly feed from your hand. The water here is shallow, clear and cooling so children of all ages will enjoy a paddle.

The Walk

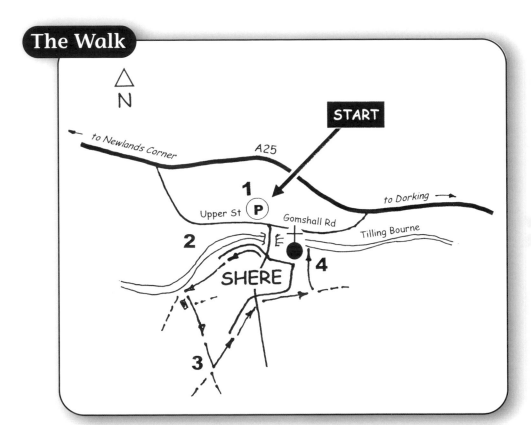

disguises its industrial use by a water company and also looks rather rustic. Ignore a ford on your right and turn left on a path that passes to the left of a house. Within yards ignore a path to your left and continue ahead between banks. The path gradually rises to higher ground and finally reaches a junction of paths by a marker post.

3 Now turn sharp left on a narrow downhill path that brings you to a quiet residential road. Continue ahead along the road to meet a road junction where you should go ahead along a lane named Spinning Walk. When the lane turns sharply left, continue ahead on a path to reach a field. Now turn left through a narrow gate and continue downhill to reach St James's church.

④ Turn right and then left and press on along a gravel path through the churchyard. Cross a bridge over the Tilling Bourne and keep ahead through a meadow to reach Gomshall Road. Turn left along the road to end this short but very pleasant circuit. Middle Street and the car park are a little way further along Gomshall Road.

DID YOU KNOW *that the Saxons named the village Scir? Since then it has variously been called Essira, Shire, Shyre, Shiere, Sheere and only became Shere during the late 18th century.*

◆ Background Notes ◆

The clear waters of the Tilling Bourne powered many mills on its short 11-mile journey from the northern flank of Leith Hill to the river Wey at Shalford. The industries it supplied included corn milling, calico bleaching, paper and gunpowder making as well as a large tannery at nearby Gomshall.

At the beginning of Middle Street there is a **well and drinking fountain** set into a wall. The water from the 280-foot deep well flowed until the 1970s but, after Thames Water sunk bore holes in the area, the water table lowered and the spring failed.

Look out for the **old jail** as you walk along Lower Street. The plaque on the wall is a fire mark and 1710 refers to the policy number not the date – the building is older.

The remains of an **anchoress's cell** can be seen on the northern wall of St James's church. She was a young girl named Christine Carpenter and in 1329, to prove her obedience to God, became walled up in a tiny cell with only a squint through which she had contact with the outside world. Her resolve failed after three years and she pleaded to the bishop to be released, which he begrudgingly did. She later begged to return and it is assumed that this time she remained until her death.

12
Ockham Common

Signals from the past

The Semaphore Tower

Can you imagine the days before telephones, how did people get messages back and forth across the country, how on earth did they manage? This glorious circuit takes you to the Admiralty's answer to the problem of communicating quickly between their headquarters in London and their battle fleet in Portsmouth. In a clearing amongst the trees dotted with picnic tables is a semaphore tower, one of a line of fifteen which continued in service until the electric telegraph was developed. This short walk is ideal for younger children as the sandy paths are gently undulating and are far away from roads. A number of seats with pretty views are placed around Ockham Common where the heather is a blaze of colour during the school summer holidays, but no matter when you visit there is plenty to see – bring a picnic.

Ockham Common

Getting there *If travelling via the M25 then take the Guildford turn-off at junction 10 and in $^1/_4$ mile turn left on a lane signed to the semaphore tower. Turn left after 250 yards into Boulder Mere car park. When travelling via the A3 take the Ockham B2039 turn-off $1^1/_4$ miles south of the motorway junction. Continue for $^3/_4$ mile before turning left at a memorial cross. Continue to a crossroads by the Black Swan pub and turn left. Ignore the first car park on your right and continue to soon meet Boulder Mere car park 250 yards before rejoining the A3.*

Length of walk $1^1/_2$ miles.
Time Allow 1 hour, more if picnicking.
Terrain Fairly level – though, soft sandy paths make it unsuitable for buggies and pushchairs.
Start/Parking Boulder Mere car park (GR 079586).
Map OS Landranger 187 Dorking & Reigate, Crawley & Horsham.
Refreshments Hot and cold snacks and drinks are available from the car park cafeteria.

◆ Fun Things to See and Do ◆

There is an abundance of wildlife across the common so see if you can identify some of their footprints in the soft sand on the paths. Look out for the tiny sand lizard that lives here – they are quite rare in England. After coming out of hibernation in March they spend the early summer months basking in the sun and preying on spiders and small beetles and even attack wasps and butterflies by laying in wait and then ambushing them.

Many fir cones will be seen along the way so why not pick up two or three and decorate them as shown in walk 14.

12

◆◆◆ ◆◆◆◆◆◆◆◆◆◆◆◆◆◆◆◆◆◆◆◆◆◆

❶ With your back to the road, pass a vehicle barrier and information boards and continue along a wide sandy path between magnificent pine trees. The route is signed by occasional posts marked with a blue arrow. In 80 yards ignore a left fork and press on ahead. At a wide crossing track by two seats and open heath, go ahead on a slowly rising sandy path to reach two more seats by another crossing track.

❷ Here go ahead and keep a roughly hewn railing to your left. Go ahead again at another crossing track and soon at the top of a short rise the semaphore

The Walk

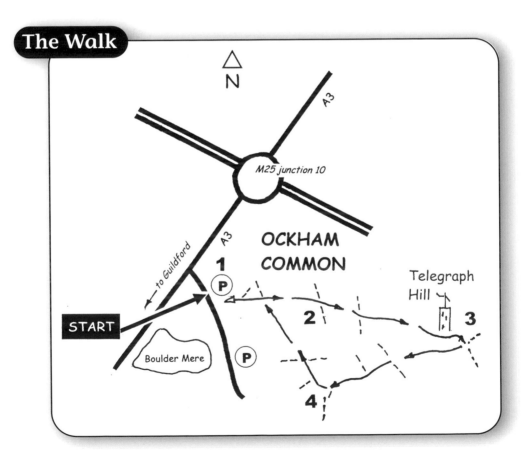

tower is reached by a wonderful clearing in the trees, the perfect spot for a picnic. Just to the left of the tower is a well that supplied the occupants with their water.

3 Leave this lovely clearing by passing to the right of the tower and continuing along a tarmac drive for 100 yards to reach a junction of paths. Now turn right on a wide bridleway that goes gently downhill and follows the line of an ancient boundary ditch and bank. Keep ahead on this track at a junction of paths by palings and soon ignore another track on your right.

4 When the track forks and ends at a wide crossing track, turn right along the crossing track. Soon ignore a track on your left and, 120 yards later at a crossing track by a post marked by a red arrow, keep ahead. After passing open heath to your right another crossing track is met by two seats, turn left here and retrace your steps through the pine woodland to the car park.

DID YOU KNOW *that it took only 45 seconds to send Greenwich Mean Time the 85 miles from London to Portsmouth via these semaphore towers?*

◆ Background Notes ◆

Chatley Heath semaphore tower was built in 1822 and was one of fifteen linking the Admiralty in London to their ships in Portsmouth harbour. The towers were positioned on high ground between 5 and 10 miles apart, with telescopes trained on the tower before and after, enabling operators to swiftly send messages back and forth from the Admiralty to their fleet. Several towers covered the Surrey section with the northernmost at Putney Heath communicating across the Thames to one at Chelsea. Next in line came those at Coombe Hill, Hinchley Wood, Chatley Heath, Pewley Down and finally one on the site of the present-day Hogs Back Hotel on the A31, which may explain the strange tower that breaks its roofline. The semaphore system finally ceased in 1847 when it was replaced by the newly developed electric telegraph.

13
Ockley

Discovering a wildlife haven

Age-old cottages look out over Ockley's village green

This exceptional circuit is full of interest for the young naturalist and is not to be missed. Beginning alongside the village green – a super picnic spot – the way follows a quiet lane that brings you to Birches Wood, a nature reserve where the path continues through the trees for almost a mile. The turning point of the circuit comes at Holbrook Farm and continues along its drive that is lined by hedgerows just teeming with wildlife. A couple of quiet lanes follow, one with extensive views over fields as far as Leith Hill in the distance before the woodland is rejoined and it is here that picturesque Vann Lake is discovered. The route is best during the summer months as the oak woodland is on clay and the path may become sticky in winter.

Ockley

◆◆◆◆◆◆◆◆◆◆◆◆◆◆◆◆◆◆◆◆◆◆◆◆◆◆◆◆◆◆◆◆◆◆

Getting there *Ockley sits astride the A29, 6 miles south of Dorking. Park in a lay-by opposite the Inn On The Green. There is additional parking 300 yards south by the cricket pitch.*

Length of walk $4^1/_2$ miles.
Time Allow $2^1/_4$ hours.
Terrain Fairly level.
Start/parking The lay-by alongside the village green opposite the Inn On The Green (GR 148403).
Map OS Landranger 187 Dorking & Reigate, Crawley & Horsham.
Refreshments The Old Bakery & Post Office, 30 yards south of the lay-by, supplies fresh sandwiches made to order and provides hot

and cold drinks. There are also two pubs facing the village green.

---

1 From the southern end of the lay-by, head away from the road on a rough track and turn left along it by a cottage. Leave the track when it soon bends right and press on alongside a pretty pond. Continue ahead on another track after passing the pond and remain on it as it skirts football and cricket pitches and swings left to pass a pavilion to meet with the A29. Cross the road and continue along Friday Street, a quiet lane that serves just a few houses. Press on along the lane and continue through a

◆ Fun Things to See and Do ◆

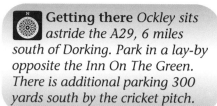

Bring a field guide with you and a pair of binoculars as there is an abundance of wildlife in the woods, hedgerows and fields that the route passes through. Things to look out for in the woods and hedgerows are squirrels, rabbits, the occasional weasel, wrens and brown hairstreak butterflies. The quiet walker may be lucky and spot a roe deer or even a muntjac deer – no bigger than a medium sized dog – grazing at the field edge while by the waterside several species of dragonfly may be seen hunting.

◆ ◆

The Walk

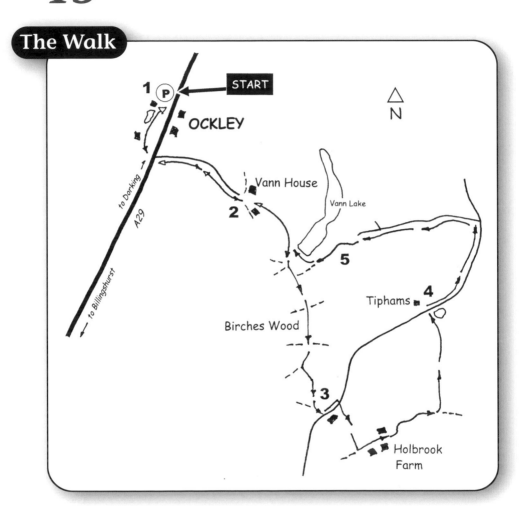

gateway by Vann Cottage to finally meet the ornate gates of Vann House.

2 Here go ahead on a fenced bridleway to the right of the gates and skirt a garden before meeting with a junction of paths at the beginning of Birches Wood. Go ahead at this junction and when the bridleway soon divides, keep to the left fork and cross a wooden bridge over a brook. In 60 yards as the path again divides, keep ahead

A charming pastoral view from the path

and ignore a left fork. Now remain on a wide bridleway that shadows an ancient bank and ditch boundary marker through the woodland. The woodland is predominately oak and has an undercover of pendulous grass that indicates a soil that will become rather waterlogged during winter. Keep ahead at a wide crossing track and again at another. When the path divides by a directional post, fork left to soon reach a T-junction with a field seen through the trees ahead of you. Go left here to soon reach a quiet lane by Weare Street Cottage.

3 Turn left along the lane and then right on a bridleway 20 yards after passing a brick building in the garden. Pass through a dip and over a stream to meet an open field where you continue ahead to the far side. Go left on a track and pass by the lovely garden of Holbrook Farm that dates from the early 16th century. The way continues along a concrete drive that is rather strangely spanned by a large barn before passing between farm buildings. Now remain on this wonderful drive for $^3/_4$ mile until it ends at a road junction by a picturesque pond.

4 Turn right along the lane which, although little used, is a public road and the occasional motorist does come this way so take care. Soon pass by a house named Tiphams, built a century later than Holbrook Farm, and press on along the lane for just over $^1/_4$ mile to reach a junction on your left with Vann Lake Road. Turn left into Vann Lake Road which again is a public road but only serves a few houses and is very quiet. Here there are fantastic views over the fields to Leith Hill where you will see its tower in the tree line. Continue on the lane until the hard surface ends by the gate to a house named Heron's March.

5 Press on downhill on a rough track through woodland and soon fork right on a signed footpath that goes down steps to meet the dam of Vann Lake. Cross a footbridge and, after 80 yards, a junction of paths is met at a directional post. Here go right on a bridleway which you met in point 2 of the circuit and follow it back to the gates of Vann House. Now press on ahead and retrace your steps along Friday Street to complete this great circuit.

DID YOU KNOW *that a lot of the village names in Surrey are Saxon? Ockley is derived from 'Occa's Lea' referring to Occa's clearing in the wood. Occa was a wealthy Saxon landowner whose estates once included this area. Surrey has more pagan village names than any other county.*

◆ Background Notes ◆

The A29 coast road alongside Ockley village green sits on Stane Street, the Roman road that linked the major Roman town Noviomagus, or Chichester as we now call it, to London. Stane Street was the shortest route between the two towns and had to overcome a few natural barriers along the way and so was not entirely straight, but there were four great sections that were extremely straight, one of which passes through Ockley. The longest straight section ran from Dorking to London Bridge and you may be surprised to know that if you travel the modern A24 road today, along its route through Ewell, Morden, Merton, Tooting, Balham and Clapham, you are following Roman Stane Street. After the departure of the Romans in AD 409, the road fell into disrepair. The Saxons had little use for the stone road but their name for stone was 'stane' and it is from them that the name Stane Street has been passed down through the centuries.

14

Friday Street

A hamlet named after a goddess

The beautiful lake at Friday Street

This lovely walk starts off in the picturesque hamlet of Friday Street, known throughout Surrey for its tranquillity. After passing the end of the pretty lake the route follows a track beside fields where rabbits may be seen grazing. Soon, a steady climb ensues and the way traverses two quiet and beautiful valleys on the northern flank of Leith Hill. Wildlife abounds as the undulating route passes through woodland and by delightful ponds and streams. Look out for a waterfall that tumbles from on high as the way brings you to the lovely hamlet of Broadmoor before climbing out of the valley on a wooded hillside to rejoin the scenic lake at Friday Street. Maybe not for the youngest of children as the circuit encompasses two short but steep hills that older children will find a great challenge.

14

Length of walk 2$^1/_4$ miles.
Time Allow 1$^1/_2$ hours.
Terrain Steeply undulating.
Start/parking Friday Street car park (GR 126458).
Map OS Landranger 187 Dorking & Reigate, Crawley & Horsham.
Refreshments The Stephan Langton pub in the hamlet.

❶ Walk to the roadside end of the car park furthest from the entrance to meet a downhill path that shadows the road. Follow it until it ends at steps. Now continue ahead down the lane to soon reach Friday Street's pretty lake.

❷ Go left on a track by a cottage below the dammed lake and soon cross a stream. To your left is a field where you have every chance of seeing rabbits grazing. Keep left at the fork by the idyllically placed High Trees cottage and keep to the wide track.

❸ At a junction of paths alongside a stone bridge over the stream, turn right and cross a

◆ Fun Things to See and Do ◆

The route passes under many fir trees and the ground is littered with cones. Why not collect some along the way and when you get home make your own Christmas decorations. You can decorate the cone with silver paint or better still, paint glue on the tips and sprinkle with glitter before it dries. Shake off the excess.

The Walk

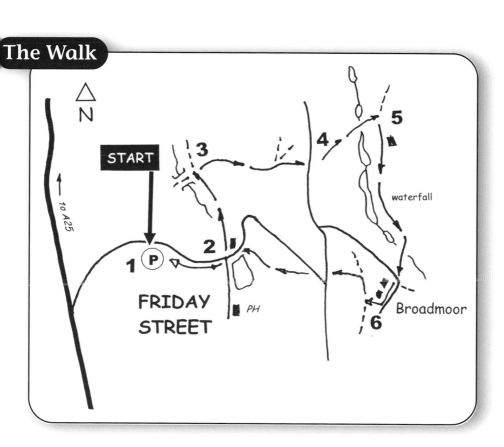

stile. Now press on ahead up a challenging and fortunately short hill between pine trees. After reaching the crest of the hill, the path divides into three. Take the right-hand path that continues by the edge of a field to soon reach a small lane.

4 Cross the lane and continue on a downhill path that soon drops quite steeply into the next valley. Pheasants are often seen in these fields and seem quite unperturbed by the occasional walker. Press on ahead at the valley bottom and pass between ponds to reach a stile at a crossing track.

5 Cross the stile and continue rightwards along this lovely track where you soon pass an isolated

The pretty hamlet of Broadmoor

house. As you near the hamlet of Broadmoor look out for a pretty woodland waterfall that tumbles into a pool to your left. Finally the track ends at a road in the hamlet and you should press on ahead ignoring a signed path to your right.

❻ Some 10 yards after passing Leith Cottage on your right, turn right on a signed footpath. At a T-junction in 50 yards turn right and pass by the rear of gardens. In 60 yards, at a fork by a marker post, bear left and follow the path through woodland as it climbs out of the valley. Maintain direction uphill to meet and cross a lane. Soon cross a second lane and continue ahead as the path descends through woodland to re-join the lake at Friday Street. For refreshment at the Stephan Langton pub, turn left at the road junction, otherwise continue ahead uphill to the car park and the end of this great walk.

Friday Street

DID YOU KNOW *that a lot of the ponds you see in Surrey are man-made just as this one is at Friday Street? Look at the end where the road is, it is a dam built many centuries ago to create a head of water to power the drop hammers of the local forge. That's why these ponds are called hammer ponds.*

◆ Background Notes ◆

It is thought that **Friday Street** derives its name from the Saxon Goddess Frigga who, in Norse mythology, was the god of love and fertility and whose name is also remembered in the day of the week, Friday.

In local folklore **Stephan Langton**, the 13th-century Archbishop of Canterbury, was born here in Friday Street and although he was a real person and did help broker the Magna Carta between King John and the barons, his birthplace is in doubt. During Victorian times, local author Martin Tupper generated the legend when he wove several Surrey beauty spots into his fictional book entitled *Steven Langton, a Romance of the Silent Pool*. Although the Silent Pool is still known by that name, its real name is Sherbourne Pond.

The pond here at Friday Street is entirely man-made and was formed by damming the infant Tilling Bourne stream to create a head of water to drive the hammers of the local iron industry. It is thought that a watermill once stood below the dam at its northern end where a couple of cottages now stand although, by the time John Rocque mapped the area in 1762, it was no longer in existence.

15
Leatherhead

Exploring the delights of the river Mole

The riverside path passes beneath this railway bridge

This walk is suitable for all, including the youngest of us, for as well as being short it offers level terrain and a great picnic spot. Starting off rather inauspiciously alongside a business park, the route follows a path beside the river and soon meets Common Meadow, a lovely open wildlife area just right for children to run around and expel their boundless energy. The shallow waters of the Mole cut through here and are suitable for supervised paddling while older children may take in a bit of bird watching, for the area is frequented by many species of bird including the green woodpecker. The return leg goes through light woodland where birds, squirrels and rabbits abound and before long the way returns to the meadow and the sparkling waters of the river Mole.

Getting there *Leatherhead is just off the M25 at junction 9. Follow the route through Leatherhead signposted to Guildford. After crossing the river Mole in Waterway Road, turn first left at a roundabout into Guildford Road and re-cross the river. The pay and display car park is to the left immediately after the bridge in Bridge Street.*

Length of walk 1^1/$_2$ miles.
Time Allow 1 hour, more if picnicking.
Terrain Level – suitable for pushchairs and buggies.
Start/parking The pay and display car park at the foot of Bridge Street (GR 164564).
Map OS Landranger 187 Dorking & Reigate, Crawley & Horsham.

Refreshments The Running Horses pub is next to the car park and further eateries can be found just a short walk along Bridge Street in the town centre.

---

1 From the entrance to the car park turn right towards the town bridge and fork right on a paved path after 25 yards. The path follows the riverbank and passes under an unusually low road bridge and two high-arched railway bridges. Press on alongside the river as it passes to the left of a modern industrial park

2 Continue through a kissing gate to enter Common Meadow – an ideal picnic spot. The river is shallow here and just right for a paddle on a hot summer's day.

◆ Fun Things to See and Do ◆

See if you can spot this strange looking plant growing on the trees as you pass through the wooded area of this circuit. It is called lichen and is quite unique as it is made up of two different micro organisms – a fungus and an alga. It grows very slowly and is a good indicator of clean air.

Kiddiwalks in Surrey

15

Ignore a right fork and continue alongside the riverbank.

3 At the end of the meadow, follow the path through trees and then swing right. Continue over a small wooden footbridge and

follow the distinct path as it curves through open woodland. There is plenty of wildlife to be seen in this lovely area.

4 After going up a low rise, a crossing path is met and you

The Walk

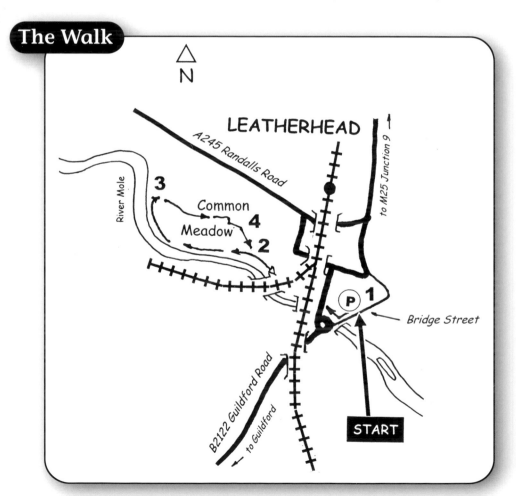

should turn right down a slope and cross another small wooden bridge to rejoin the wildlife meadow. Turn immediately left along the woodland edge and soon, at a crossing path, bear right and make for the kissing gate in the corner of the meadow. Now, simply retrace your steps along the riverbank to rejoin the town bridge from where the circuit started.

DID YOU KNOW *that the river Mole used to be called the river Emlyn? The name Emlyn is derived from Y-Melyn – old English for mill. The name Mole is not named, as was fancifully believed in the 17th century, for its habit of disappearing down swallow holes in dry years but from 'mola' – again, meaning mill.*

◆ Background Notes ◆

The business park near the beginning of the circuit is on the site of the Ronson cigarette lighter factory. Ronson, for so many years the producer of petrol lighters, were the first to launch the revolutionary butane gas lighter in 1954 with the 'Premier Varaflame' at the top of the range. All came with a choice of cases including leather and suede that reflected the fashion of the day. The company unfortunately had long standing financial difficulties and Ronson UK went into liquidation during 1981.

Common Meadow dates back to the 17th century and, although Leatherhead's other commons where enclosed in 1860, Common Meadow escaped enclosure and horses and sheep remained free to graze. The Ronson factory used the meadow as its sports ground between 1950 and the 1970s. The Lower Mole Countryside Management Project has successfully improved the area for both wildlife and the public.

16

Reigate and Colley Hills

A bird's eye view of Surrey

The shorter route is suitable for buggies.

This walk begins on top of Reigate Hill and follows the North Downs Way long-distance path through beech woodland before emerging on the open hillside of Colley Hill beside what locals call the 'Temple', once a drinking fountain but now a toposcope. The full route continues through Margery Wood where, in springtime, the woodland floor is awash with bluebells and their characteristic scent hangs in the air. After circling the woodland, the path brings you back to the escarpment of the North Downs where, on clear days, there are fabulous views across the Surrey Weald as far as the South Downs in the distance. The panoramic views, short grasses of the hilltop and well-placed seats make this lovely place the perfect picnic spot.

Reigate and Colley Hills

Getting there *The walk starts from the car park to the east side of the A217 at the top of Reigate Hill and ¹/₄ mile south of junction 8 of the M25.*

Length of walk 2 or 4 miles.
Time Allow 1 or 2 hours.
Terrain Gently undulating. The shorter walk is suitable for pushchairs and buggies.
Start/parking National Trust free car park on top of Reigate Hill (GR 263523).
Map OS Landranger 187 Dorking & Reigate, Crawley & Horsham.
Refreshments There is a refreshment cabin in the Reigate Hill National Trust car park that serves simple hot and cold snacks.

1 From the car park, pass to the left of the refreshment cabin and cross a footbridge over the A217. Now continue along the well-trodden track that forms a part of the North Downs Way long-distance footpath. Press on ahead at a small lane and very soon pass Reigate Fort on your left. The route continues ahead along the well-defined track where there are still obvious signs of the 1987 Great Storm that wrecked havoc in the south-east. Finally the track brings you to the open hillside of Colley Hill beside the 'Temple'. It is here that the shorter route can end so, if that is your option, enjoy the views before you retrace your steps back to the car park.

◆ Fun Things to See and Do ◆

On a clear day there are bird's-eye views across the Weald as far as the South Downs. Bring a pair of binoculars to help in spotting aircraft taking off and landing at Gatwick airport some 8 miles away, as the crow flies, or, nearer still, try to spot the sails of the old windmill on Reigate Heath less than 2 miles away.

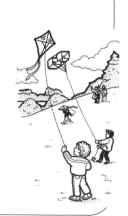

The up draught from the steep escarpment here makes Colley Hill a fine place to fly a kite but be careful not to go too near the edge!

Kiddiwalks in Surrey

16

The Walk

2 The full route continues along the track that is set back from the escarpment edge. Some 20 yards after passing Colley Hill's landmark water tower on your right, turn right through a gate to reach a footbridge that crosses the M25. Press on through Margery Wood on a well-trodden path to reach a car park.

3 Make your way to the car park entrance by Margery Wood Lane. Turn left here and in 4 yards turn left again along a bridleway that runs along the woodland edge. When Laurel Cottage is reached, continue over a lane and soon

turn left along a second lane. Pass by a lovely cottage named Thornymoor, that sits behind a uniquely cut hedge, and press on to re-cross the M25. Ignore drives to left and right and continue ahead passing two coal duty posts to reach a signed bridleway.

4 Turn left here through woodland on a well trodden path to reach a gateway that leads onto the open hillside of Colley Hill.

5 Pass through the gate and bear right alongside a fence to reach the edge of the escarpment.

Reigate and Colley Hills

◆◆◆◆◆◆◆◆◆◆◆◆◆◆◆◆◆◆◆◆◆◆◆◆◆◆◆◆◆◆

Ignore a gate to your right and follow the escarpment leftwards passing some well-placed seats to finally arrive back at the 'Temple'. Retrace your steps along the North Downs Way to complete this great walk.

DID YOU KNOW *that the bluebell was used as a starch for stiffening collars during medieval times? Never trample bluebells as they rely on healthy leaves to produce the following year's bulbs.*

◆ Background Notes ◆

Near the beginning of the walk the route passes **Reigate Fort**, one of several built on the North Downs during the Napoleonic Wars. They were never intended as truly defensive positions, but rather as mobilisation centres that could supply guns and ammunition rapidly to troops which had dug-in along the hilltop in the event of a French invasion. In 1906, with the threat of invasion over, the forts were closed down although, much later, Canadian soldiers occupied this one during the Second World War. The next fort westwards is on top of Box Hill, and another one that I know of in Surrey is Henley Fort, high up on the Hogs Back above Guildford. It later served as a Surrey schools' camp and, in the late 1950s, my schoolfriends and I enjoyed a memorable holiday there.

The **coal duty posts** seen on the longer route once served as boundary markers that indicated where duty on coal became payable on its journey to London. The tax was originally raised to help in the rebuilding of London after the Great Fire of 1666 and ceased only in Victorian times.

A small herd of **belted Galloway cattle** are sometimes used by the National Trust on Colley Hill to help keep the scrub down to manageable levels. These small hardy cattle with their attractive panda markings also assist in conservation grazing programmes at Oxted and in West Sussex.

17

Outwood

Discovering Britain's oldest working windmill

The working windmill at Outwood Common

This circuit starts from the heights of Outwood Common that itself makes an ideal picnic spot. Leaving the common behind, the route sets off along a quiet drive and soon reaches farmland where the way continues through pretty scenery on easily followed field paths with far reaching views. Hedgerows line the way and just teem with wildlife during spring and summer while a little later in the year there is an exquisite banquet to be had from the massed blackberries. The route turns and passes through a shallow valley where a small brook is crossed before continuing on to its furthest point by Burstow Park Farm. The return route is over more pretty fields to rejoin the outward leg that now climbs easily back towards Outwood Common and the old mill.

◆ ◆

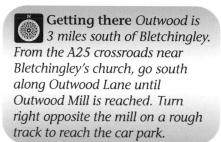

Getting there *Outwood is 3 miles south of Bletchingley. From the A25 crossroads near Bletchingley's church, go south along Outwood Lane until Outwood Mill is reached. Turn right opposite the mill on a rough track to reach the car park.*

Length of walk 2³/₄ miles.
Time Allow 1¹/₂ hours.
Terrain Gently undulating.
Start/parking National Trust free car park on Outwood Common (GR 327456).
Map OS Landranger 187 Dorking & Reigate, Crawley & Horsham.

Refreshments The Bell Inn is a few yards north of the mill and offers good refreshment.

❶ From the car park, walk 25 yards back towards the road and then go left across the open grassy area where you pass by the garden of a house named the Chapter House. At the end of its garden, bear left to reach a quiet drive where you go past a pretty row of cottages and Windmill Garage. Continue along the drive and ignore a right fork. When the drive ends by a couple of cottages, press on ahead through trees to meet with a stile at a field edge.

◆ Fun Things to See and Do ◆

Why not visit Outwood windmill where, if the wind is favourable, you can see the mill producing flour just as it has for over 300 years. There is a small museum, and ducks, geese and sheep roam the area. There is also a small children's play area.

The windmill is open to the public every Sunday between 2 pm and 6 pm from Easter Sunday until the end of October.

2 Cross the stile and continue ahead over a meadow to reach a marker post by the corner of a long field. Now with a hedgerow on your left, continue ahead until you finally reach a stile ahead of you between two oak trees.

3 Cross the stile, and ignoring paths ahead and to the right, turn left here and follow a field edge as the path continues into a shallow valley and crosses a brook to reach a stile. Cross this and keep ahead as the path

The Walk

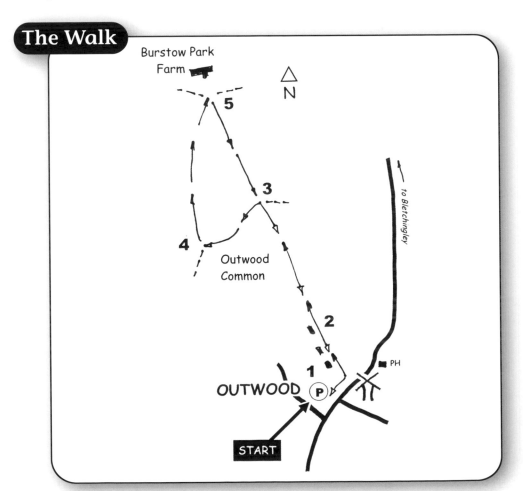

climbs easily to reach a stile in the corner of the field.

4 Cross the stile to meet a bridleway and now turn right and follow it through fields towards farm buildings with a backdrop of the North Downs beyond. Finally a junction of paths is met by the farm track of Burstow Park Farm.

5 The way now turns sharp right over a stile where you continue through gently rising fields towards a hedgerow with the stile between two oak trees that was met earlier at the end of point 2. Here press on ahead and retrace your steps back to Outwood Common to complete this enjoyable and picturesque circuit.

DID YOU KNOW *that the post mills that survive today are almost identical in design to those built in medieval times? The only real difference is the brick-built roundhouse at the foot of the later mills that offers additional dry storage.*

◆ Background Notes ◆

Outwood windmill is the oldest working windmill in Britain although nowadays it produces only small quantities of flour for visitors. Being a post mill means that the entire 25 tons of its wooden structure is supported on one single huge central oak post and it is so finely balanced that it only requires one person to turn it around to face into the wind. Thomas Budgen from nearby Nutfield built the mill in 1665 and local tradition says that villagers climbed to the roof a year later to watch the flames of the Great Fire of London burning some 22 miles away.

In 1790 the then owner's brother built a much larger eight-sided smock mill next to it as a rival but the venture turned out to be less than successful and it never got the better of the old mill. The smock mill ceased working in 1914 and soon became dilapidated with its final indignity coming in 1962 when it collapsed during a storm.

18
Bletchingley
From the heights of Castle Hill

Surveying the scene from Castle Hill across to the Weald.

This pretty field-path walk begins with extensive views over the Weald where, on a clear day, aircraft will be seen taking off and landing at Gatwick Airport while a little nearer is Redhill airfield where privateers fly. Beginning on the high ground of Castle Hill, the way soon descends to meet level fields that are home to flocks of sheep tending their young lambs during springtime. As the way progresses eastwards the route continues along peaceful field paths lined with hedgerows just brimming with wildlife so there is always plenty to see for budding young naturalists. As the circuit begins its return to Bletchingley, it climbs surprisingly easily across fields to rejoin the high ground and the end of this lovely circuit.

Bletchingley

 Getting there *Bletchingley sits astride the A25 between Redhill and Godstone.*

Length of walk $3^1/_4$ miles.
Time Allow 2 hours.
Terrain After descending Castle Hill, the route is level although the last mile rises 200 feet without much notice.
Start/parking The service road off the A25,150 yards west of the Red Lion pub at the western end of the village (GR 322507).
Map OS Landranger 187 Dorking & Reigate, Crawley & Horsham.
Refreshments The Red Lion pub at the beginning of the circuit.

❶ Walk eastwards alongside the A25 to meet the Red Lion pub. Here cross the road and continue, to reach Castle Square. Turn right into Castle Square and at its end carry on along a narrow path signed GW (Greensands Way long-distance path). The path now skirts the earthworks of Bletchingley Castle and there are fantastic views over the Weald. Continue on this fenced path as it descends Castle Hill to finally arrive at a stile by a farm track.

❷ Cross the stile and continue left to reach a junction of tracks after 60 yards. Ignore a track on

◆ Fun Things to See and Do ◆

 Bring a pair of binoculars with you as Redhill airfield is not far away and small aircraft, including old bi-planes, are often seen flying quite low over the fields along the route. A little further off, much larger craft will be spotted taking off and landing at Gatwick.

If you are interested in nature, then bring along a small wildflower field guide to help identify the many plants you will see along the way. The tiny scarlet pimpernel can be seen flowering along the route only on sunny days, which gives rise to its country name of Poor Man's Weather-glass.

18

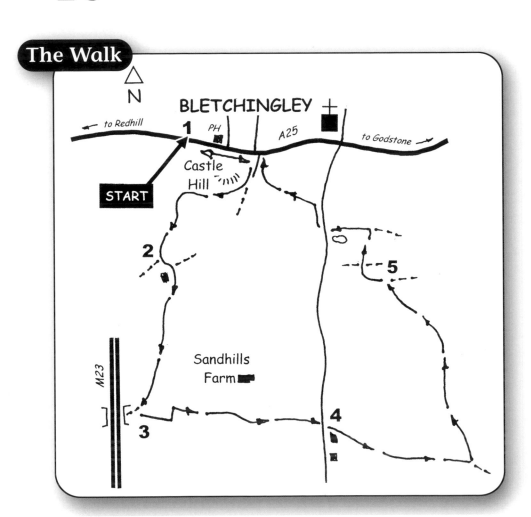

your left and continue ahead to pass barns to meet a stile by a gate. Cross this and now follow a peaceful cart track through two large fields, ignoring a track on your left at a second stile.

❸ The track heads for the M23 and, when it bends sharp right 100 yards before meeting the motorway, cross the stile ahead of you. Turn left and follow the field edge to reach and cross another

An inquisitive local

stile in its corner. Bear left and in 60 yards continue rightwards alongside a boundary fence. Go over a stile in a line of trees ahead and continue alongside the next field edge. Press on past some woodland, at the end of which cross a stile on your left. Bear right to meet the top left corner of a field where you cross a farm bridge and a stile. Now continue ahead to cross a stile at a road just left of a cottage.

❹ Continue on a bridleway opposite and pass by a large arable field to enter woodland. Some 10 yards before the end of the woodland, seek out and follow a narrow well trodden path on your left. Cross a brook and continue along the woodland edge to reach a field. Cross the field diagonally left to reach a marker post by a gap in a hedgerow. Pass through the gap, turn right and continue alongside the field with a hedgerow on your right. At the end of this field cross a stile and bear left through a second field and enter woodland. Keep to the well-worn path through this pretty bluebell wood to reach another field where you press on to the far side to meet with a T-junction.

❺ Turn left here on a path that passes between banks to reach a junction of tracks. Go ahead on a rising path that passes between fields to reach another T-junction. Turn left on the path marked GW and stay on the main track to pass a secluded pond to reach a road. Turn right alongside the road to reach the pavement. Look out for an electricity sub-station on your left. Here go left and continue on a fenced path to rejoin Castle Square where, by turning right to meet the A25, the end of this great circuit is met.

18

DID YOU KNOW *that Bletchingley was known as a 'rotten' borough? Up until the Reform Bill was passed in 1832 the village was able to send two elected members to parliament with just a handful of votes.*

◆ Background Notes ◆

The route starts near the indistinct remains of Bletchingley Castle that lie on private ground and are hidden by a dense covering of trees, although the path near the beginning of the circuit circumnavigates the large earthworks. The Normans built the motte and bailey castle soon after the Battle of Hastings and as you will see from looking to the weald below, it held a commanding position. A motte and bailey castle consists of a deep ditch (the motte) that surrounds a mound (bailey) topped with either wooden or stone ramparts.

It was the home of Roger de Clare who during 1170 was visited by Hugh de Morville, Reginald Fitz Urse, William de Tracy and Richard le Bret; four knights who had overheard a furious King Henry II berate Archbishop of Canterbury Becket's independent views. They were on their way to Canterbury to demand that Becket tow the line and pardon men he had previously excommunicated. They found Becket in the cathedral and when he refused their demands they hacked him to death with their swords - an event that stunned the Christian world and led to Becket's canonisation. The penance of the four knights was to serve with the Knights Templars in the Holy Land for 14 years while King Henry, who had belatedly tried to stop them meeting Becket, was to supply 200 knights for a year in the defence of Jerusalem and vowed to the Pope that he would spend 3 years on crusade himself – which he never did.

19
Woldingham

Discovering the 'Pilgrims' Way'

A well-placed seat on the North Downs Way

This energetic walk is through rolling countryside that has been described as 'little Switzerland' and, although there are no mountains, the undulating circuit will be a challenge for children. Starting off in Great Church Wood nature reserve, there is plenty to see and many wildflowers to identify along the way as the path drops easily down into a valley. Here a pleasant driveway leads you along the rising valley floor with great views on either side. After meeting the North Downs Way long-distance path, a climb brings you to the top of a ridge where there are panoramic views and seats that make it the perfect picnic spot. The way now continues along an ancient track, adopted by the long-distance path, and stays along the high ground to rejoin the nature reserve and meet the end of this splendid circuit.

Getting there *Take the B269 south from Warlingham. In 3 miles pass Botley Hill Farmhouse pub to meet a road junction with the B2024 on your left. Turn right here on a road called The Ridge and signed to Woldingham. After 1¹/₄ miles, when the road bends sharply right, turn left into Gangers Hill and the car park will be seen on your right in ¹/₄ mile.*

Length of walk 3¹/₄ miles.
Time Allow 2 hours, more if picnicking.
Terrain Undulating.

Start/parking Car park in Great Church Wood nature reserve (GR 373541).
Map OS Landranger 187 Dorking & Reigate, Crawley & Horsham.
Refreshments Botley Hill Farmhouse pub on the B269.

---

❶ Pass through a gate marked 'Woodland Trust' and soon, ignoring a wide track on your left, go ahead on a gently sloping downhill path through woodland that offers great views across the valley. Stay on this path and ignore a finger post pointing right into woodland. Pass by a seat

◆ Fun Things to See and Do ◆

 Make an attractive sculpture by collecting an interestingly shaped leaf , ensuring that it has prominent veins on its underside. When you get home, cover a flat surface with greaseproof paper and roll out a piece of children's modelling dough to about 5mm thick and slightly larger than the leaf. Place the leaf vein side down on it and roller it. Now cut around the leaf with a plastic knife and then peel the leaf away from the dough. For a permanent sculpture use Das modelling clay which air-dries and hardens in two days.

The Walk

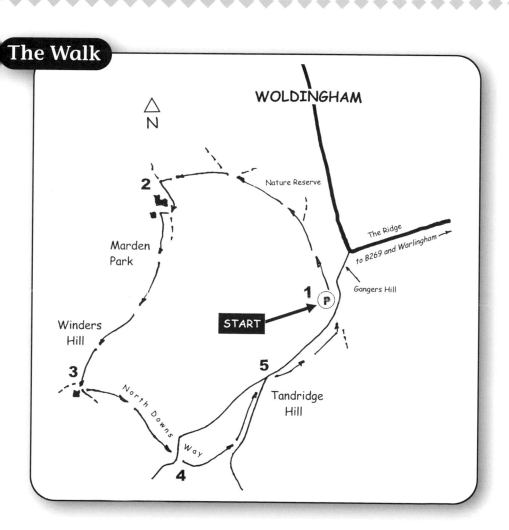

offering a great panorama over the valley and continue, soon meeting a junction of paths with a field gate ahead. Go left, soon ignoring a right turn signed to Woldingham Station.

2 When the path meets a T-junction by a gate marked private, turn left on a wide track to soon meet school buildings. At a T-junction ignore a stile ahead of you and turn right along the

There are great views along the way

tarmac drive to a second T-junction with a cottage opposite. Turn left here through ornate iron gates and continue along a wonderful drive that follows the valley floor.

❸ When finally a vehicle barrier is met by a cottage, fork left on a narrow path signed as the North Downs Way. The way now climbs to the top of the ridge and passes a very welcome seat along the way. Stay on the long-distance path, which is marked by an acorn sign, and pass through wonderful beech and oak woodland to meet a country lane by Hanging Wood Farm.

❹ Go over the lane on the marked path that now drops down to a second lane. Follow the path as it gains height and shadows the lane before finally meeting it, where you continue for 30 yards to meet a road junction.

❺ Go right alongside the road for 120 yards before forking right along the North Downs Way path. At a junction of paths follow the acorn sign right and then left and pass by a couple of seats with panoramic views. In 180 yards, when the long-distance path turns sharply right, go left up steps to meet the road with the car park beyond where this fantastic circuit sadly ends.

DID YOU KNOW *that a butterfly differs from a moth mainly by its caterpillar forming a hard chrysalis rather than a soft cocoon? The other distinct difference is that the butterfly has antennae that look like a thread with a knotted end while the moth's antennae look rather like a feather.*

◆ Background Notes ◆

Much of the walk is through Marden Park which was created during the 17th century by Sir Robert Clayton, a wealthy London banker and one-time lord mayor of London. A rundown farmhouse was replaced by a luxurious mansion and he set about creating walled gardens and plantations of trees that included walnuts. Many influential people visited here including John Evelyn, the diarist, and William Wilberforce, the slavery abolitionist. Sadly the house was totally destroyed by fire in 1879 and has now been replaced with the present brick mansion which is a part of Woldingham School.

The circuit, from point 5, follows an ancient trackway known to have been made by Mesolithic man. There has long been a track along the top of the North Downs which provided easier travel for those on foot or horseback from the winter mires of the Weald below, but it is purely a Victorian notion that pilgrims on their way to Canterbury followed this path and in fact it was their early mapmakers who first romantically labelled it as the 'Pilgrims' Way'. In reality there were many routes through Surrey that took in villages that are mainly below the escarpment where pilgrims would have sought out food and shelter.

20
Crowhurst

Discovering Britain's oldest tree

Crowhurst's 4,000-year-old yew tree

This pretty walk starts from St George's churchyard where an old hollowed-out yew tree has lived since the Bronze Age. Although it has been recorded that a table and chairs were installed during Victorian times that seated twelve people, they must have been mighty small – take a peek inside and see what you think. After leaving the old tree behind, the way crosses fields with lovely views and reaches a pretty piece of indigenous woodland where the circuit turns southwards to reach the buildings of Stocks and Kingswood Farms. The way then follows a pleasant farm track that offers easy walking with good views and brings you back to Crowhurst where the route crosses fields to re-join St George's and the end of this pleasant stroll.

Getting there *Crowhurst is easiest reached via Lingfield. From the eastern side of Lingfield, go north on Station Road until it ends at a T-junction in 1 mile. Turn right for 20 yards and then left into Crowhurst Road where, after a further 2 miles, St George's church is reached on your left. Park at the roadside.*

Length of walk 1³/₄ miles.
Time Allow 1 hour.
Terrain Level field paths.
Start/parking By St George's churchyard, Crowhurst (GR 391475).
Map OS Landranger 187 Dorking & Reigate, Crawley & Horsham.
Refreshments There are all the usual eateries in Lingfield's High Street.

◆ Fun Things to See and Do ◆

 Older children might like to make a simple tool for measuring the height of trees. Draw a centre line along a short length of wood. Hammer in a nail on the line at each end and one in the centre. Using sticky tape, attach a protractor under the centre nail. Now tie a weighted piece of string to the centre nail and your tool is ready.

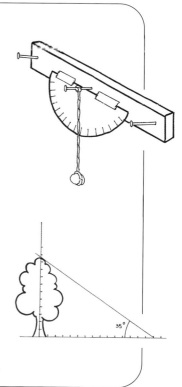

Pace away from the tree you wish to measure – say 20 paces – and look along the three nails to the top of the tree and write down the angle that the string is indicating. When you get home, draw two lines at 90° and mark out a scale, in this case make 20 marks at say 10 cm intervals on each of the lines. Now with your protractor draw a line at the angle you wrote down earlier and this will give you the height in paces. Armed with the measurement of your pace you can now work out the tree height.

1 Pass through the lych gate of St George's church, where you will see ahead of you the famous old yew tree. The route goes to the left of the church along a gravel path to a kissing gate. Continue along the top edge of a field, passing an idyllic cottage that has enviable views over the countryside. Press on along the top edge of three more fields to reach peaceful woodland.

2 Maintain direction through the woodland until a marker post is reached 20 yards before

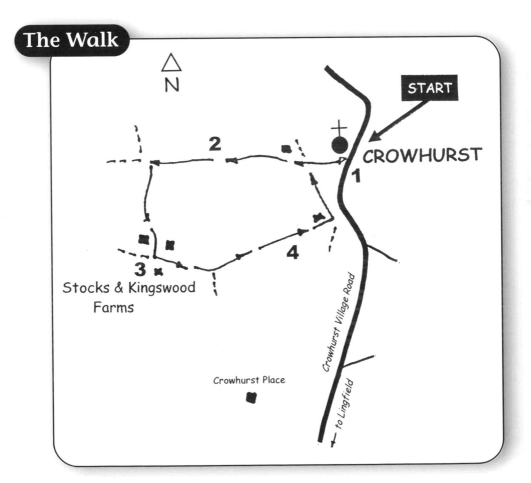

The Walk

N

2

CROWHURST

1

3

Stocks & Kingswood Farms

4

Crowhurst Village Road

to Lingfield

Crowhurst Place

A pretty field path with the spire of St George's church in the distance

the woodland ends. Here turn left on a narrower path between the trees to eventually reach and cross a stile and enter a field with farm buildings ahead of you. Cross the field to the far left-hand corner where you go through a gate and continue alongside the buildings to reach a T-junction with a farm track.

3 Turn left along the farm track and pass between a couple of houses. Keep ahead on the track that is bordered by hedgerows but, at a junction by an open field, bear left. Once again you will have open views across the fields and will now be able to see Crowhurst Place, one of Surrey's most important buildings. The moated house was built in the early 15th century for the Gaynesford family who have fine tombs inside St George's church. To the left of the house is a massive dovecote dating from around 1910 when the house itself underwent skilful restoration by

Kiddiwalks in Surrey

20

George Crawley for the Duchess of Marlborough.

❹ Continue along the farm track and pass by barns to reach a marker post with a road in view beyond. Turn left over a stile and cross a couple of small fields in a straight line to meet and cross a stile half hidden in a hedgerow ahead of you. Finally cross a third field to meet with your outward path by the scenic cottage you passed earlier. Now turn right to re-join St George's churchyard where an internal viewing of the church is well worthwhile.

DID YOU KNOW *that in 1650 the girth of the old yew tree measured 9.35m while by 1984, some 344 years later it had only added another 33cm?*

◆ Background Notes ◆

The tiny hamlet of Crowhurst has its claim to fame in the old yew tree in St George's churchyard. The church itself is Norman in origin and contains memorials to the Gaynesford family who occupied Crowhurst Place just across the fields between the 14th and the 17th centuries. Although many ancient yew trees are dotted around Surrey, this is the granddaddy of them all. While some years ago it was believed to be 1,500 years old, the consensus of modern opinion dates it to around 4,000 years of age – just imagine, it was a sapling during the Bronze Age.

During 1820 locals hollowed out the centre of the trunk and found a Civil War cannonball embedded in it. By Victorian times the tree had became a curiosity and a table and chairs large enough to seat 12 people were installed and it is even rumoured that Queen Victoria herself once visited.